# Roadkill on the
# Information Highway

# Roadkill on the Information Highway

*Steven A. Ludsin*

Writers Club Press
San Jose New York Lincoln Shanghai

# Roadkill on the Information Highway

Writers Club Press
an imprint of iUniverse.com, Inc.

For information address:
iUniverse.com, Inc.
620 North 48th Street, Suite 201
Lincoln, NE 68504-3467
www.iuniverse.com

ISBN: 0-595-14571-X

Printed in the United States of America

# INTRODUCTION

Sovereign Impunity
September 1998
My Money, Money & Business
The New York Times
229 West 43$^{rd}$ Street
New York, New York 10036
Re: Small Business Administration, My Disappointment

To the Editor:

I was thrilled to see the possibility of publishing my first-person account of the 5 years of experience with the U.S. Small Business Administration, the federal agency mandated by Congress to aid, counsel, assist and protect the interests of small business. I had the simple idea of selling the SBA's real estate collateral for defaulted small business loans on the Bloomberg.

After law school, I began my investment banking career in 1976 and Michael R. Bloomberg was one of the partners in charge that I answered to. In 1985 I purchased a home from foreclosure in East Hampton, NY. I began to pursue the concept of selling foreclosures on computers soon after I purchased the home. I tried to get a Small Business Investment Research grant from the Department of Commerce but was turned down. When the S&L bailout began in 1989, I brought the idea of electronic marketing on the Bloomberg to the RTC, the agency in charge of the bailout, but I could not get a contract.

Undaunted I persisted and received a good audience with Erskine B. Bowles, currently the Chief of Staff of the White House. In 1993 he was the Administrator of the US Small Business Administration.

I convinced the SBA to give me a pilot program in 1994 to sell the real estate collateral on the Bloomberg. After enduring the frustration of the contract renewal process, I managed to get the contract renewed in June 1995. Battling the SBA has become almost a full time job; it has sapped my financial resources and has resulted in a seemingly endless litigation process.

My story of this struggle should alert your readers to the idea that one should be careful about what you want because you might get it. I had to use the Freedom of Information Act to get the appraisals of the properties the SBA hired me to sell because they claimed the contract did not provide for giving appraisals. Then they insisted on charging $10,250 for the processing fee which was discretionary. The SBA decided I was a commercial requester so I had to pay the fees. I challenged the decision in the Federal Courts in New York and actually presented my own oral argument before the Second Circuit Court of Appeals. The 3 judge panel told me I was at the top of the list of attorneys who have appeared on their own behalf, but the Appeals Court held that the SBA could charge me the fee because my contract goals were not in the public interest. So even though I was selling federal assets and disseminating the information world wide on the Bloomberg, I had to pay the SBA the FOIA fee. A friend from a prominent midtown law firm assisted me in filing a writ of certiorari with the US Supreme Court.

I was able to get the appraisals and present them to investors by displaying the photos and descriptions and scanning the full appraisals using my own scanner. I finally received bids from 2 major investment banks but after 2 years into the second contract beginning in June 1995, the SBA had forgotten to tell me that they would need consent of the lending banks to sell the assets in bulk which was my goal under the contract. There is a breach of contract claim pending before the General Services Board of Contract Appeals and the hearing is scheduled for December 7, 1998. The claim is for $1.2 to $2.4 million for providing buyers ready, willing and able.

I share this account of my struggle because it is a microcosm of the cultural rift of the private sector and our federal government. Your readers should look before they leap and get involved with entrepreneurial ideas to try to make money with the government as a contractor. Ironically the SBA is selling $10 billion of assets in the coming years. How could they seriously believe the private sector would participate if the agency doesn't understand the marketplace and thwarts any innovation at every turn?

Very truly yours,
Steven A. Ludsin
The writer is a lawyer and investment adviser

# CONTENTS

# ECONOCIDE

Robin O. Clay died. I assumed he died of Aids but it turns out he had brain cancer. He probably died on December 1, 1998 which was exactly 5 years from the day I received the yes from Erskine B. Bowles, the Administrator of the SBA, the acronym for the United States Small Business Administration. Erskine ultimately became chief of staff in the White House.

Robin O. Clay was my COTR, Contracting Officer Technical Representative. He was the person responsible for the day to day implementation of my contract. This story begins with his death and my rebirth.

The Small Business Administration is a quaint anachronism that was created in 1953. I was a toddler then and somehow my growth was more substantial than theirs was. I believe the agency is there for propaganda purposes. An interest group that embodies American capitalism that every elected official supports because you can't be against small business. Now the good intentions of the creators have been perverted by the current senior career officials. I am not referring to the political appointees. I am referring to the career people. They do not have any appreciation of business risk. Given that warm send up let me tell you how I became roadkill on the information highway. I was hoodwinked into believing they meant to help entrepreneurs but in fact they kill any idea that might lead to profit for someone who came from outside the agency, i.e. reality.

# ECOMMERCE BEFORE IT'S TIME

I had been frustrated in my attempts to get a research grant in 1988 when I sought a Small Business Innovative Research Grant from the Department of Commerce. My idea was to increase the liquidity of distressed government real estate, given the upcoming economic decline. I was prescient. The S&L crisis followed and the use of an automated database of assets was created to help unload the Resolution Trust Corporation's portfolio.

After getting jerked around by the RTC for 5 years, I had a bureaucratic moment where you get to politely tell the person who has been your obstacle to stick it as they say. Lamar C. Kelly Jr. had no desire to let me sell the RTC's assets on the Bloomberg, and he would take the attitude of produce and we'll talk, but it was hard to be taken seriously without a contract.

# TELL YOUR STORY

As I write this story there are many skeptics that tell me no one would care about this story. As always I remain the contrarian and believe that the indifference and hostility I encountered is the same reaction that mere mortals receive if they don't hire lawyers or professionals to run interference for them. I believed the Clinton Administration was committed to improving the delivery of services by Federal Agencies and they probably still do, but there is little incentive for federal employees to do anything different unless there is a crisis. Then if you create a crisis, they demonize you for not being a go along, get along person. I describe the process by using a radiation analogy. First they x-ray you to death and then they say you're too radioactive to deal with.

I feel abused by the myopia of the emulators. I call the SBA senior career officials the emulators because they emulate the worst kind of stereotype of indifferent, incompetent government employees and they are proud of it. Think of those old horror movies like the Body Snatchers with bodies being used as channels for alien life forms. The emulators have been channeled by those old country dogs sitting on the porch in the heat, drooling and half asleep.

Okay, the SBA career people didn't drool, but they were frequently half asleep.

The irony is watching the impeachment of President Clinton for a conspiracy of crimes to obstruct justice. Ironically Eric Benderson, the SBA's Associate General Counsel in charge of litigation asked me at a pre trial conference for the Freedom of Information Act (FOIA) claim (for the appraisals of the properties they hired me to sell but wanted to charge me a $10,250 fee for), whether I thought there was a conspiracy against me. My quick response was that I didn't want to waste any mental energy to even think about it. The fact is that there was a conspiracy to sabotage my sales efforts to keep the delay mode in place indefinitely. For purposes of telling this story let's just call it the cabal. It is easier to get studies as to how much the excess assets and loans will command in the marketplace as opposed to actually selling them. The SBA's current sales program includes the basic approaches I suggested like making the appraisals available, creating due diligence documents, putting the data on cd's or other computer media, but they refused to let me earn the million dollar commission.

The depositions in my breach of contract claims created wonderful revisionist history renditions by the emulators. One of my favorites was Arnold S. Rosenthal, in charge of portfolio management and sales, who said with a straight face that a bulk sale is 2 properties. The premise of my effort was to sell the portfolio in bulk as in 150 properties or more, not 2. The belligerence and stupidity was astounding. For example, in April of 1996 in a meeting in DC Arnold Rosenthal said I should try to sell the properties that I had information on. In other words instead of being able to sell the whole portfolio in an intelligent manner, I should content myself with the arbitrary portfolio of properties that happened to have some photos and appraisal excerpts, or should I say scraps, and therefore be grateful for their further arbitrary conduct. This agency is basically not accountable.

# THE LAGOON

In my mind a lagoon is a dark place filled with mysterious creatures that are probably harmful to your health. The SBA was a lagoon. The resistance of the lagoon isn't rational so that when people ask me why they were so unconscionable in their behavior I don't have an answer. I always speculate that they wanted me to evaporate after the pilot program and were particularly pissed off when I managed to get a piece in the Washington Post called Citizen Burned by SBA with Hot Idea. After that, I finally got the renewal of the marketing contract with a $50,000 retainer against a 2% to 4% commission. So I would have earned about $1.4 to 2.8 million if there was a 70 million dollar transaction and the emulators didn't want any part of that.

It is so hard to convey the atmosphere of a meeting with people who are only going through the motions. It's kind of like dating a woman and spending money on her, when she knows she's never going to sleep with you but she enjoys the strokes. You certainly feel the hostility but their basic numbness makes it appear that you may be making progress in gaining acceptance of your ideas. In some ways you are like entertainment, providing a diversion from their offices stacked with documents and phone messages that are probably not going to be returned. The more I think about it, the more I imagine the SBA has become very similar to the military. The form of thinking about strategy and executing plans is there but not the substance. As long as the Congress can be made to think the small business agenda is being met, the rest of the community is basically irrelevant. As the SBA's General Counsel once told me, the Congress and the press can work against you, when you use either pressure source to accomplish your goals, and yet that was the only way I was able to get my train back on track. I lobbied Congress and managed to get the Washington Post Article in April 1995.

The lesson of the litigation is that you are in an inherent position of weakness, since the government attorneys have unlimited funds and time is meaningless to them. In addition, they are so programmed in their response that it is usually the same no matter what the facts are. I recall the tactic of exaggeration was a regular method. Gary Fox was a seasoned practitioner. Fox was the kind of person that was slammed against the locker in high school and probably went home crying. So he got his revenge of the nerd by becoming a miserable human being and using that misery to make litigation a torture chamber. He sat for hours, never drinking water and just trying to pervert your responses to trap you into saying something that he could use against you at trial. He tried to raise a kind of domino effect theory to create fear that the SBA would be besieged if the goal I set out for myself was met. For example, when I was trying to explain the marketing approach I took and how I wrote down names of a wide cross section of people or companies I solicited in my travels he would jump in with the hysterical fear that I could have put down everyone in the phone book and they would not have known the difference. I immediately thought how absurd this reaction was and yet it was their tactic to exaggerate and belittle your legitimate efforts by overstating the worst case scenario and creating fears that were groundless. I guess that's the way Fox would have marketed, opening the phone book and dialing everyone. Even he might have succeeded due to the law of averages.

His assistant, David Fishman was a great example of the emulator syndrome. He looked up to Benderson and Fox, both of whom would have been at home in Argentina during the military regime handling disappearing persons. Then again he had to look up to them because he was also shorter than they were. I enjoyed David Fishman's business experience background. He was the junior attorney I dealt with most often. As compared to Benderson and Fox he wasn't as offensive, which is kind of like saying Goebbels was more pleasant than Himmler was. They resented the comparison, but I think these attorneys abuse their position as advocates and are really integrated into a system that repels outsiders and only makes it appear that they are doing anything constructive. As long as they can keep the Senate and House Small Business Committees away from their doorstep, the rest is easy.

So there is Fishman trying to impress me with his business and marketing experience: he worked in a Men's Store in Southern New Jersey and did some of the accounting. I practically laughed in his face, but he was serious. It would be like me trying to be a pilot when the closest I ever got to the controls of a plane is when I used the men's room closest to the cockpit. At least I flushed the toilet.

# Structural Impediment

The sheer brazenness of the emulators was embodied in their withholding the fact that they needed the consent of the lenders in order to do a bulk sale. Here I was after 2 years and 5 months into the second contract and they drop this bomb at the negotiating table when we met at the offices of the Carlyle Group. As Richard Gluck, one of the lawyers that worked with me put it, there were structural impediments. He had been providing legal advice in the litigation and moral support. He was incisive and quick on the uptake. I nicknamed him laser mind. I was trying to use the litigation as a club to beat them into submission and come to the table to negotiate a sale. Since the lagoon wasn't going to cooperate on its own, I was able to get some response when the Chief Judge, Stephen M. Daniels at the Board of Contract Appeals would order them to provide documents about the Woodmont study or encourage them to talk about settlement. But delay was the tactic used to the hilt by the lagoon lawyers, just run the clock and the rest takes care of itself.

Reinventing Government

The Woodmont Study was a theoretical analysis about what the SBA would recover when they sold their inventory. The woman who did the study was an RTC veteran and a consultant. Essentially her work helped the lagoon remain in their miasma for another year waiting for the results that would guide them into the marketplace as if they didn't have a clue as to what their inventory was worth. They probably didn't have a clue, but it is hard to believe that they didn't accumulate some sense of value over the years.

When the matters that involve your agency involve less than a billion in DC, you can fly below the radar screen and no one really cares what you do as long as you leave a paper trail for the auditors and oversight committees or agencies. So the General Accounting Office does a study exposing the fact that there are few cost controls or concerns about return on the sale of assets and the conclusions recommend changes. So the agency sets up a few new teams to address the problem and then its back to business as usual. That's reinvention of government. Take your lashes, heal your wounds and then go back and do the same things with a few studies to roll out in case someone follows up and wonders what the study was supposed to improve upon. When you have unlimited money and no sense of time, it's the only way to go.

# MLK Jr. Day 1999

Marking time from Martin Luther Kings day is appropriate. I usually tried to regain momentum after the New Year. In retrospect the only thing the senior career officials responded to was crisis. Unfortunately if you created a crisis in order to get some movement you would be demonized for disrupting the status quo. The clever means by which they maintain the status quo was to hire new contractors to take more years to accomplish the same goal. Once you decide to sell assets why do you add more time to take to achieve your goal? It helps keep your job. The taxpayers have little interest in your work so the charade continues. Now that the clock starts for the 10 billion dollar asset sale, it will be years. So instead of criticizing, its time for me to monetize, going through the contracting gauntlet was very costly. It is possible to turn this into money since reform is virtually impossible, but perseverance isn't.

# ROBIN CLAY IS DEAD

I had mixed feelings about the death of Robin O. Clay. Part of me feels sorry for the sadness of his death. On the other hand I feel that there is a form of revenge and that the death should be the beginning of a plague on their house. The venality of the core group that tries to keep the operation under their constant control is deep and pervasive. After all, they have spent their careers using and abusing the process to create the illusion of assisting small business, but the reality is a system favoring their own folks. I recall meeting the Colson Services group or the vendors at a small business expo in Washington. There was a quiet reaction trying to assure that only the faithful had a real slice of the pie. The ritual of meetings and appearing to be interested was only a formality. Once a decision was made to use certain firms or individuals, you were protected.

I arrived unannounced and from the top. The resentment was palpable, but I thought a breath of fresh air would be exhilarating. How foolish I was. The cabal had strict membership requirements and it was handled quietly and secretly. Naturally, the methodology is so ingrained that denial of its existence comes easily. You can spend an hour listening to someone with a good idea and then give that idea to your preferred list and hire him or her to do it. Of course you can expect a spot for yourself at this newly expanded firm once you decided that you were ready for the private sector. Keep in mind if the budget involves less than a billion dollars in Washington, there is little interest in spending time on searching for abuses and the system perpetuates itself unabated.

# SELF PRESERVATION

I thought about the agenda of the emulators and self-preservation ranks first. The asset sale they are now planning is taking the usual snail's pace. The selection of the strategic advisor known as the program financial advisor finally happened in January 1999. Now the Transaction Financial Advisor will be selected for the first sale by January 21, 1999. Of course another 6 months will pass just to put together the first sale which keeps the lagoon in place for a long time to come. Anything under a billion dollars doesn't matter. It is a familiar mantra once you repeat it. I find the prospect of a sale of 10 billion dollars in loans to have immense appeal.

The smoke screen will remain in place since there are new players in the loan sale. To these newcomers the procrastination seems natural. It is systemic and calculated to stall for its own sake. I recall Chief Judge of the General Services Board of Contract Appeals Stephen M. Daniels sage observation just because the SBA staff is stupid and they don't like you doesn't mean there was bad faith. I thought that was a good start to show bad faith but the standard of acceptable conduct is so low that the SBA can do what it pleases and keep flying below the radar screen.

The more I think about 10 billion dollars in assets the more excited I become. I was getting educated on the basics of the loan program and now we've reached the mother lode. The ineptitude continues. The Transaction Financial Analyst was supposed to be chosen by close of business on Tuesday January 20, 1999 and when I tried to call the three people in the Procurement and Grants management Office about the selection there was no one available. Reform is out of the question, so the time has come to capitalize on their incompetence. Why didn't I think of that sooner? The worse they are in getting things done the better it is for the buyers. Just keep showing up and someday the odds will favor us.

# CENTRAL CASTING

I am revolted when I see the image of the staff I dealt with at SBA. I could name each player but suffice it to say that central casting could not have done a better job. I also noticed that there was no sign of Administrator Alvarez to be found at the 1999 State of the Union message and she has not been mentioned in the press. So the Secret Business Administration continues and no one cares except the people who make the loans or receive the loans. I guess the need for my name in lights has changed to the benefit of keeping a lower profile. The only time the whale gets harpooned is when it swims close to the surface. The greater the amount of the sale the lower the publicity. It all makes sense now. Whatever I once believed has changed and I have to do a 180-degree turn and look at it from the opposite side. The persons that give you a short term negative can make the situation positive if you stay the course. They count on you leaving, so we'll continue to follow the proceedings.

The Transaction Financial Advisor was chosen. After being told the announcement would be made at the close of business, I reminded the Procurement spokesperson that he said the same thing 2 days before. So he confessed and told me it was KPMG Peat Marwick LLP in DC. I put a call through and after being referred to the Library I called back and got a real person's voice mail from the Government Contract Division. I then dialed the next highest number and spoke to a person hoteling at the office. It sounded like a homeless business person which is what that verb describes. The person is only occupying an office that isn't there. I finally spoke with another Government contracting person who kindly agreed to find the right person and forward my fax which I sent after our phone conversation.

The Program Financial Advisor relayed the exaggerated claim of the SBA staff that I sued them in 14 states in 14 different ways. I said that wasn't true and he asked whether there were any lawsuits. I told him that I already informed him of the FOIA claims and that they were not supposed to give out negative information. So the alienation I am experiencing in an effort to subcontract leads me to the position that I am better off working with the buyers. The harder the SBA pushes away, the positive reaction is to work with the buyers. There couldn't be any ethical issues in my case since it is unlikely I will participate in the sale. Nevertheless I did receive a response from KPMG and that was a pleasant surprise.

# FILES FROM HELL

The difficulty of looking around my room and seeing all the files and documents is extreme. Consequently I refuse to abandon the whole effort to market government assets, particularly SBA assets, because I learned too much and that knowledge has value. I am always impressed with the polite and rapid response from the private sector contractors. Quite a contrast to the government officials who continue to delay the inevitable by reciting the mantra, No decision yet, close of business today, or Should have an answer next week. Most people walk away but this is part of my being now, so stay tuned for the unfolding saga. I will continue to contact the private sector sales transaction financial advisors in order to keep abreast of the proceedings and the timetable. I assume they will figure out a way not to subcontract so I'll be the buyers' bird dog.

I decided to keep the marketing division active. The rest of the government contractors seem to be able to take no for an answer. Then again they are operating in collectives, so it's easier to win a few and lose a few. I keep reminding myself that god shuts one door and opens another. So the buy side becomes more inviting, but strategically I need to appear that I am looking for the subcontract just to become part of the loop. Contrary signals can be helpful. I also find it energizing to speak to the caliber of companies that are seeking the contracts. They are by and large polite and willing to listen to intelligent ideas as opposed to the threat you become when you deal with the senior government career officials. Emphasis on the word career. It is difficult to put yourself in the shoes of these status quo thinkers, but I guess its instinctive to protect your turf by any means you can get away with in spite of federal regulations that say otherwise. That's sovereign impunity. You are in charge and no one will successfully challenge your position, you just add more rocks to throw over the walls to the attackers down below.

# PHOTO OPS

I was able to revisit a simple concept. A picture's worth a thousand words. Fortunately, technology enables the budding filmmaker to create video images of still photos and capture them in the computer and then shoot them back to a video for commercial application. After seeing those images so often perhaps I can begin to understand why the SBA was so attached to them. It's like playing monopoly on the poorer streets.

# BULBOUS BENDERSON

U.S., unscrupulous scum, that's what comes to mind when I think of the Associate General Counsel for Litigation, Eric S. Benderson. He has a bulbous face with shifty eyes and he is long passed the point where he thinks integrity is even an issue. The continual manipulation of the process to keep a cabal in charge of the commercial interaction with the private sector is his specialty. It is easy to perpetuate since they choose new outside contractors who either go along or they don't get a piece of the pie. On paper the right procedures are followed, but a pre-determined outcome manages to emerge. I didn't realize the competitive nature of government contracting so to the extent I managed to get 2 unsolicited proposals to be adopted because the idea was unique, innovative and original is increasingly more remarkable as I look back on the contracting experience.

# Video Colpur

I have been told that I should play up my creative side. I found it liberating to create the video of the Colpur properties. It is a handy marketing tool and not too costly to reproduce. I tracked down the first Transaction Financial Advisors, KPMG in DC. I got a polite reception from Shelly Klein and a follow up from Bob Schmid who gave me the proverbial we'll keep it on file. Nevertheless I think I can provide value added to the buyers by developing diplomatic relations with the transaction financial advisors. The SBA has boxed me out of the subcontracting opportunities for now, but the contractors create teams for other tasks they bid on, so it is incumbent upon me to keep the marketing option open with the contractors. You don't ask, you don't get.

# Foreclosure Dreams

In order to give perspective to the state of things in 1999 I must recount the process which in hindsight was set up to hit the glass ceiling. It all began in 1985 when I heard about a foreclosure sale in East Hampton, New York. I managed to get the sales contract and when I went to the courthouse I realized no one came except me. As I walked along the beach in East Hampton I had an epiphany. Why not try to use computers to market foreclosures? I approached Michael R. Bloomberg, who was my first boss at Salomon Brothers, and asked if he would let me use the Bloomberg Financial Markets System to market foreclosures. His reaction was skeptical. How do you stop someone from saying they didn't see the offering on the Bloomberg instead of the newspaper and therefore I would be screwed as a broker? I waited but the idea wouldn't go away. When the RTC (Resolution Trust Corporation, the government agency in charge of the Savings and Loan bailout), came along I thought my dreams came true.

The inspiration for computer marketing came from the purchase of my home. The reality of dealing with the RTC came from the devil. The game was they picked whom they wanted to and ignored who they wanted to and by the time you could effectively challenged the decisions they evaporated. Great modus operandi. As Gary Bowen, one of the first RTC staff members said, Steve Ludsin's been here since the days before we had trashcans. He's now with the FDIC in Hartford, Connecticut and ironically I might sell a Manhattan Condo to a Bloomberg employee that came out of the FDIC portfolio I recently updated on the Bloomberg. I heard the FDIC office closed in Hartford so Gary Bowen probably has new trashcans again.

The earliest meetings in September 1989 were quaint in terms of the lack of structure. I had a positive encounter with a lawyer, Carl A. Polvinale. He was in charge of marketing when I met him and his decisiveness and businessman's approach encouraged me. Unfortunately he was moved into Ethics and Conflicts and marketing ended up in the hands of Lamar C. Kelly Jr. and Thomas Horton. Lamar was like a southern sheriff, outwardly congenial but his eyes gave him away as the shrewd card player he was. Thomas Horton boasted to the Wall Street Journal that he had never sold any real estate during his career and now he was selling 17 billion dollars of real estate. Doesn't that say it all? Ironically Tom Horton has been a consultant to the SBA for its bulk sales. This is a potentially problematic situation since the SBA needs as little encouragement for the foot dragging and indecision that was the RTC's approach.

# ASAP

I also met Carl Polvinale's friend and assistant John Dolan. I tried to keep the concept alive and even got an acronym (ASAP) for the Automated Sales Action Program assigned to the idea by a wonderful staff person, Robert Montagne. I never got a contract to market RTC's assets, but I actually sold about $600,000 of condos in Amityville, NY.

I will never forget the meeting on July 1, 1993 when I had just returned from Latvia. My father and I joined a group of Jewish Holocaust survivors on a trip to Latvia. We had regained title to 3 buildings that my grandfather owned since 1918 and we hadn't had title since 1941.

So I walked into a meeting with Lamar C. Kelly Jr., the head of asset sales, Robert Montagne, who had named my program ASAP and a young woman who was the Congressional Liaison. I was joined by Matt Schneider a Washington lawyer who I went to Cornell with and William Montalto of the Senate Small Business Committee. Lamar kicked of the meeting with the warm opener, We thought you died. I responded that not only did I not die, but that I was sure Lamar realized the Holocaust Museum had just

27

opened that past April 1993 and that I was a member of the Presidential Panel that built the Museum and the only child of a survivor on the group. I added that I just returned from Latvia and regained title to the 3 properties my grandfather owned since 1918 and that took 52 years, so I guess I had time don't I Lamar? I never saw a contract from the RTC but it felt good to have that interaction with Lamar. Kind of a thank you note in your face.

# No Man's Land

The RTC experience taught me a few lessons. I guess I should have walked away, but my survivor genes told me to forge ahead. I would be remiss if I didn't tell the story of my first road trip to get a contract from the regional office of RTC, which was originally in Red Hill, Pennsylvania. It was the Friday after Thanksgiving and I called the head of the office. I arranged to visit the following week. I was received by a curious looking fellow with deep-set eyes and a permanent look of being slightly hung over. He was fairly receptive and even announced at one point that I would be their person in New York, or some such overstatement.

I was encouraged, but it turned out that the proclamation never went beyond that point. I will never forget the fact that Red Hill,Pa. was so remote that there were no restaurants open for lunch. I ended up in Allentown at an ersatz Bavarian Garden spot with food to match. It should have alerted me to the pitfalls of dealing with this agency, but I thought I fell into a positive opportunity. It turns out the fellow with the permanent hangover must have been in serious emotional pain, since he attempted suicide and failed and then tried again and succeeded. The regional office was moved to Valley Forge, Pa. and I understand that 2 more staff people including one attorney also committed suicide. I had piqued the interest of a Wall Street Journal reporter with the 3 suicides story but nothing was ever written. Similarly in 1997 I had a piece about the intransigence of the SBA in negotiating with my buyers about to run in the enterprise section of the Wall Street Journal, but the editors pulled. I assumed they contacted the former Wall Street Journal reporter who joined the SBA and she put the freeze on it.

# CLINTON FOR PRESIDENT

The election of President Clinton changed the landscape for me. I had worked on the campaign as a spokesperson in the Jewish community supporting Clinton. It was the easiest speech to make, since President Bush remained a distant figure to the Jewish community. I remember telling President Clinton how proud I was that he was the President on the opening day of the Holocaust Museum. The point is it was a labor of love working to get Bush out and Clinton in. When Clinton was elected I decided to try to profit by getting a position in the White House or a contract. I conceived an Office of Small Business Liaison for which I was eminently qualified. The Office of Small Business Liaison was folded into the Office of Public Liaison. I realized the only move was to approach Erskine B. Bowles the SBA Administrator to help me get the ASAP program jump-started with the RTC. I had met with Roger C. Altman, Deputy Secretary of Treasury to get the Lamar Kelly meeting, but once I was in the SBA I realized I might have a better shot at getting a contract to sell the defaulted real estate of the SBA on the Bloomberg.

# TURN AROUND IS FAIR PLAY

In May 1993, I was granted a meeting with Erskine B. Bowles to discuss what efforts he might expend to help me with the RTC and my attempt to get a marketing contract. The RTC gave out something like 1 billion dollars worth of contracts ranging from security services to asset managers. While I was waiting for the meeting with Erskine, I picked up a brochure about the National Resources Sales Assistance Program. It discussed the propaganda about all the wonderful things the SBA does for America. It included a section about how the SBA helps get set asides of minerals, timber, oil and other commodities from government programs. It mentioned that SBA did not have title to any of these assets except for real estate from defaulted loans held as collateral known as Colpur. I should have known by the sound of the expression Colpur, which stood for collateral purchased, that it would be an invitation to disaster. After all it sound like something that would involve the Balkans like Kosovo or Herzogovina. Ambassador Holbrooke held meetings of rival factions in Colpur near the border of Serbia.

# TIME WARP

---

I met with Erskine and he was a breath of fresh air. I spent an hour with him, which in Washington time is about a week. In fact after taking the Amtrak to DC for so many years I realized you are going into a time warp when you leave New York, A New York minute is equal to one month in DC. So according to my calculations, the hour I spent with Erskine is equal to 60 months, which would be 5 years. That is the time it took for this saga to unfold or more accurately to implode.

In the interest of clarity I found the chronology I created for a Congressional Staff member of the House Government Reform and Oversight Committee. There was a period when I believed the Office of Small Business Liaison was a possibility. I recall the meeting that evolved in New Paltz, N.Y., I had returned from the Inaugural and maintained a sense of urgency, mission, purpose and most of all opportunity. I felt that the formation of the new White House was seat of the pants it terms of its structure. In other words, the campaign staff scratch and claw to get a good position and arbitrary decisions are made, but you have to buy the ticket as they say in the lottery.

# KILLER INSTINCT

The thought occurred to me that I have the killer instinct inasmuch as I did not feel much sympathy for the death of Robin O. Clay. He did the SBA's bidding and made my life as difficult as possible. I feel slightly embarrassed by the sense of satisfaction that there will be a plague on their house. It is a clear case of abuse of power when career personnel use the process to abort initiatives because they envied the potential success of the contractor. The commission of 2 to 4 percent of a bulk transaction was too much for them to bear, that would have been 1.4 to 2.4 million dollars. I have enjoyed reading a new book about the 48 Rules of Power in which the authors discuss the need for surrender to lull the enemy into complacency and then strike when they aren't prepared. I harbor the resentment and look forward to the unraveling of the cabal that exists in the SBA headed by Eric S. Benderson, an amoral vestige of government mediocrity that flourishes when no one bothers to examine the machinations of an agency that falls below the radar screen. Remember anything less than a billion dollars in Washington is meaningless.

# New Paltz FDR Country

Returning to the aftermath of the New Paltz encounter I recall the window of opportunity that I had with President Clinton to discuss his economic program. When he left the auditorium I approached him and explained I was the fellow that was sending materials about the need for an Office of Small Business Liaison. He looked slightly taken aback as he emerged from the room, but I proceeded to explain that I knew Bob Rubin, (Head of the National Economic Council and hen Secretary of Treasury) and Roger Altman (Deputy Secretary of Treasury) and I gave him my letter from Mack McClarty (Chief of Staff). He took the letter and put it in his suit jacket inner pocket.

I had a dark blue suit on and my Arkansas flag pin in my lapel. I followed the entourage to the gym where the students were cheering the President and then I trailed the group into a small classroom for a private reception with the President. I was running on adrenaline at that point. I went up to the President and apologized because my giving him the documents may have made him feel I was serving him with a summons and complaint. I said that I thought the way he outlined the sacrifice by the average citizen in order to bring down the deficit helped to gain acceptance of the plan. He nodded and looked at my lapel pin and commented that he liked my pin. That became a theme between us in the coming months.

I left New Paltz on a tremendous high and I genuinely believed that the face time I had with the President gave my ideas the chance for acceptance. I tried to persuade Bob Rubin, who was then the Chairman of the National Economic Council, that the Office of Small Business Liaison was a sound idea. I even had a meeting in his office down the hall from the Oval Office. In any event, the Administration decided to let the head of the SBA do what I thought the Office of Small Business Liaison should do.

Undaunted, I had a meeting with Mark Middleton in the White House because he was copied on a letter that was sent to Erskine B. Bowles from Mack McClarty. Ultimately I met with Erskine and he was the first person to truly support my electronic asset marketing on the Bloomberg. It was a meeting that ended on a positive note with Erskine escorting me to the door and I looked up to him and said, This is the beginning of a beautiful friendship. Little did I know that I was up against an infrastructure at SBA that emulated the law enforcement in Casablanca, Round up the usual suspects.

# ERSKINE THE WASP WITH A HEART

I proceeded to fax various follow-ups and forget me nots to Erskine. Coincidentally, a high school acquaintance became Deputy General Counsel of SBA. When he told Erskine he knew me since high school, Erskine responded that Steve Ludsin was the most aggressive guy he knew. I didn't think it was an insult.

# STAFF IDENTITY GAME

In July 1993 I had the first meeting with a SBA staff person. He seemed reasonable, but after I made my pitch at the Bloomberg offices in D.C. he informed me that he was the wrong person to speak with and I should meet with Charles Hertzberg. So I said let's call him and set something up. I didn't realize this was the usual, gee I'm not the right person, so come back next trip, which we hope you won't make, but if you do, we have stalled the clock so that if you last long enough maybe something might actually happen, but if things go according to plan you'll be history, a slight blip on the radar screen.

Undaunted I met with Hertzberg and that was getting closer to the pace of thought and activity at the SBA. Arteriosclerosis is a fair diagnosis. It was as if cholesterol of the brain was a genetic qualifier for employment.

# REPO MAN

After my presentation to Chuck Hertzberg I allowed for 2 weeks to try to get a response. That is the equivalent of taking the Concorde to Chicago in terms of SBA time conversion charts. Remember a good rule of thumb is that a New York minute takes a month in Washington, D.C.

I received a predictable and scary response. We reviewed your proposal and 2 others and we rejected all of them. Yours was the highest cost and one was free. Those words screamed in my ear like cymbals smashed together in my ear. They rejected a free offer? I immediately faxed a letter to Erskine asking him to invoke his discretion permitted under the statute and reconsider Hertzberg's decision. That was on a Friday. By Monday Hertzberg was given early retirement. I don't know if my experience had anything to do with it, but I wasn't unhappy. The exasperating part of dealing with the SBA is the glacial indecision that has little to do with policy and mostly to do with ass covering. Don't decide, keep your job, don't rock the boat and preserve your retirement by running the clock. God bless America. The agency supposedly helping small business is basically a credit enhancement for borrowers with a legion of public relations efforts to convince entrepreneurs that they have a sympathetic ear at the SBA. It just ain't so. Think Small Business Abomination.

# MY DADDY SAID IT DOESN'T GET BETTER THAN YES

After continuous reminders to Erskine's office, I finally got my yes on December 1, 1993. As Erskine said, his daddy had a saying, it doesn't get better than yes. I remember the meeting in Rick Hernandez's office. It was Erskine, Rick (Counselor to the Administrator) and Larry Barrett, a staff person from Information Resources and Management or a similar euphemism. In any event I am facing the three of them and something inside tried to break the tension, so I blurted out, we have a wasp, a Latino, a black and a Jew, how could we go wrong? They all laughed since the early days of the Clinton Administration emphasized the diversity of participation in the new Administration. Basically I was told I had the pilot program for 6 months and $25,000. I later discovered that the threshold for small purchases without competitive bidding was $25,000 although it was raised to $100,000 soon thereafter.

I left with the sense that the ball would start rolling. I was assigned to Billy Jenkins in the procurement office. He was a friendly person who would raise his eyebrows when I made some hopeful statements. In retrospect I realize that he was a part of the business as usual mentality that is the SBA. The concept of change is so foreign that the approach of the staff was if you ignore something long enough it will die. I also had a COTR, the contracting technical representative, named Jane P. Butler. She was a matronly efficient person. Basically humorless, although I did see her dressed as a clown for a holiday and that was a highpoint. She was tolerant during the pilot program, but I'm sure she was happy when it ended and she did little to suggest the right path I should take. When I took her deposition during the breach of contract discovery phase, I recall my shocked reaction that the staff called one office to check the viability of the bid from Carlyle Group. One office out of approximately 65 countrywide. And why did they choose the one office? It was Los Angeles and they had an accelerated sales program as part of a Liquidation Improvement Program. They sent a swat team headed by a staff person from Maine, who probably liquidated 2 properties a year. I was never let down in the low expectation scale. When I thought the level of incompetence had reached a low point, a new fact would confirm that there was no floor on the low expectation scale. In the spirit of government I will refer to the Index as the LES.

# Pilot Program

The pilot program was deemed to begin when I received the data, which was April 22, 1994. Bear in mind I got the yes on December 1, 1993, so 5 months was not considered to be a delay from the SBA's standpoint. From my perspective I recall the frustration of getting a response and I used a variety of excuses to call and get results. I would always attend the Holocaust Commemoration events in April, which was one of the events I used to convey the idea I would be in town, so why not button things up? It was similar to the dripping water on the boulder effect. If you kept dripping someday you would penetrate the rock.

I held a conference call with Diane Gannon and Frederick Klein, Jr. of the SBA Office of Information Management. Diane coordinated the computer system and she was cooperative. Rick Klein was doing his job and didn't have much to do with my receiving the data, but he was a colleague of Larry Barrett who helped me shepherd the pilot program to its infancy. Generally these folks were cooperative, and they were also peripheral to the real goal which was to sell the assets described in the data. I think alluded to would be a better characterization of the data than description.

# BLOOMBERG ASSISTANCE

I returned to New York and met with John Loza of Bloomberg to review the raw data in anticipation of breaking the items down into a readable database. John was helpful in opening up the database and letting users sort according to State. I spent a lot of effort just getting the information out there. I didn't realize the limitations placed on me by the skeletal quality of the descriptions, but I forged ahead thinking I could improve upon it as I went along.

When we were ready to launch I spoke with Jane Butler and faxed her the language for the announcement on the Bloomberg Financial Markets System worldwide. I was pleased that there was finally some tangible progress. The perfunctory response from Jane Butler should have alerted me to the basic indifference they had to the project. They placated me hoping that ultimately it would be business as usual. I had kept my enthusiasm since I believed I was reinventing government and invigorating the process with new approaches. In retrospect I was a management consultant with a small portfolio that would be filed in the tomorrow file assuming tomorrow ever came. I was the skunk at the picnic, but just as they say in poker if you don't know who the sucker is at the table, its you.

# CENTRAL CASTING

---

The cast of characters in this corner of the SBA was direct from central casting. Earl Chambers has 2 hearing aids and I'm not sure whether they were to tune out what he didn't want to hear or selectively turn up the volume when it suited his whim. I remember speaking with him in front of the office building containing the SBA. I felt like Mike Wallace of 60 Minutes trying not to offend but not shrinking from expressing my opinion, which was not eagerly received by Chambers.

# Augment Not Preempt

---

Prior to the pilot program I was ushered into a meeting with Earl Chambers, Granville Craddock, John Cox and Larry Barrett. Chambers cut to the chase at one point and asked me whether I was saying that they weren't doing their job. I responded involuntarily and instinctively that I wasn't there to preempt them, I was there to augment them.

I was improvising as the contract began. Their attitude was only reactive. I initiated and they agreed since what I was proposing only scratched the surface. The fact that the SBA would need to get the consent of the lenders in order to sell in bulk was never addressed during the pilot program of 1994 or the 1995 contract. That was their ace in the hole to kill the chance I had to make a 2% to 4% commission. Eric S. Benderson, Associate General Counsel of Litigation and the true behind the scenes manipulator of the whole liquidation group, was so pleased with himself when he could drop that bomb on the Carlyle Group on October 16, 1997. Always keep your killer pill until the end. I would have become impoverished if I went the marathon to the trial, but I hope and believe their duplicity and unethical conduct will be revealed.

# MISSISSIPPI BURNING

The attitude was like the one depicted in Mississippi Burning. We don't want no outsiders telling us how to deal with our nigger problem. In the movie the FBI sent a team of investigators to find the bodies of 3 civil rights workers. The pilot program did not involve anything nearly as controversial, but the attitude that the tail doesn't wag the SBA dog, and you must let sleeping dogs lie, permeated the entire relationship if one could call it that.

After seeing the movie Civil Action and the A&E special featuring the real life people I felt a similar sense of frustration and the sinking feeling that the truth is at the bottom of the bottomless pit, quoting the attorney for Beatrice Foods. The same smugness was exhibited by the SBA attorneys since their money wasn't on the line and their time was paid for. The SBA flies below the radar screen in Washington. Anything less than a billion is small potatoes in Washington. Although SBA guarantees billions in small business loans, the annual budget is small in Washington scale. Consequently, the oversight is mostly in form. The occasional GAO study documenting their incompetence and then recommendations which will be implemented at least for a few weeks. In other words, the SBA stays in its own time warp, which is somewhere around the early sixties. Keep the forms filled out, and repel any innovations.

# SBIC Swamp

A classic backwater in the lagoon that is the SBA is the SBIC program. SBIC stands for Small Business Investment Corporations. These entities act as government sponsored venture capital investors. The SBA ends up owning the assets of these SBICs when they are mismanaged. Liquidating those assets is even more problematic since the basket is so mixed. Warrants, stock, real estate, machinery and equipment, etc. comprise the leftovers. The folks in charge are not too dynamic. Tom Morris is the classic nerd. Colorless and emotion free. I remember chatting with him during the furlough in 1995. He was friendly and seemed stress free, primarily because few people realized the SBIC program existed and there appeared to be few demands placed on him. George Corey was an underling who tried to emit business signals but it was only on the surface. He was eager to try my liquidation ideas if it was free, but by the time anyone made a decision, I took the position that the terms should be the same for that division as it was for the Colpur liquidators. That was the last chance for that initiative. Somehow the SBIC people thought it was a great honor to be able to work for them for free.

In retrospect the intransigence of these individuals makes sense. If you know that your goal is too hold on to business as usual, you will do nothing to allow a new idea to flourish. Consequently the sucker at the poker table plays his cards only to come up short since the deck is stacked. I recall the dietary habits of the Colpur liquidators. Apparently the generation that preceded the current group would try to find the cheapest places to have lunch. To the extent diet affects the brain cells I think the Food and Drug Administration could have a field day with these specimens.

# GENERATIONS

The next generation emulates their predecessors. Thus David A. Fishman, the junior attorney for litigation takes on the duplicitous traits of Eric S. Benderson the senior attorney in the group and Gary Fox the next man down from Benderson. They act as if it was their money they were spending. On the other hand Benderson pushed the ethical envelope when he helped to create entities to liquidate assets without going through the usual procurement route. Now the emulators figured a new strategy, procrastination. Just keep program decisions from being decided and life will remain static.

The emulators have their own code and modus operandi. Basically they will hold meetings and keep logs, but nothing new happens unless you virtually move to Washington. Whenever you visit DC the first question asked of you is how long are you here for? The only intelligent answer is indefinitely. Otherwise the emulators can ignore you because soon you'll be gone.

# SKELETONS

The first batch of data on the Bloomberg was a step in the right direction, but it was skeletal at best. I assumed I could gather information from the field offices or the brokers but that was a narrow pipeline. It was difficult to get supplementary information about the properties and the existence of the pilot program was probably dismissed as a novelty as part of the new kids on the block coming with the Clinton Administration. John Loza, the programmer at Bloomberg was able to use the RTC database as a prototype so we were operational fairly soon.

I order to announce the SBA pilot program I had to get approval from Jane Butler. I also set up a meeting with Jane Butler built around the annual Holocaust commemoration ceremonies. I remember calling her at home in Baltimore and she was quite taken aback. I explained that I wanted to be sure I was on her agenda. I recall a story I heard from someone regarding her husband. Apparently he was clowning around with some friends and they drove a car with him on the hood. He fell off and suffered head injuries which let to serious amnesia. This in turn gave Jane

Butler serious headaches. I wasn't too encouraged by this infor-mation, but you have to play the cards that are dealt to you.

Since I was improvising as I went along, I found myself reading a variety of news articles and government publications. I also perused mailers from the American Enterprise Institute or the Telecommuting in Action Seminar. I reviewed the Pentagon's Advanced Projects Research Agency and the National Institute of Standards and Technology. I was trying to find some input and avoid reinventing the wheel. If I had really been getting coopera-tion from the SBA, it would have been possible to operate in tan-dem, but I was like those petri dishes in chemistry lab that you left in the dark and watched what bacteria would grow if left alone. It must be a vestige of all those years of experiments by the govern-ment on unsuspecting victims. Once you enter the funhouse, be ready for the surprises. The biggest surprise to me was the lack of input or suggestions. I would propose and they would approve. Unfortunately, my learning curve was so steep, that by the time I comprehended the operation the 6 months would be over, and that's just the way they wanted it.

# Monthly Report

I would submit a monthly report due by the 5th day of the month. The excerpt would look like this:

May 3 94 Tuesday

Established target date of Tuesday May 10 for the release of the data on the Bloomberg. Spoke with John Loza to review improvement of selection method of sorting Colpur based on property type.

May 4 94 Wednesday

Discussion with Billy Jenkins to arrange for submission of the invoice. Met with John Loza at Bloomberg to see the data to be released on Tuesday May 10.

I would also speak with potential purchasers to anticipate announcement of the program. I was concerned as to how to finance the whole effort. I befriended a fellow named Ira Davidson of the Small Business Development Center to discuss plans for bank financing. He was very cooperative. His role was to work through Pace University and support small business. There were offices and seminars, but it was more of a propaganda arm with some hands on assistance. Federal funds are spent to allow interested parties to say they are assisting that sector, even though the actual benefits were remote and cosmetic.

I made the mistake of using RTC Go as the entry on the Bloomberg to access the properties for sale. I asked Erskine if SBA Go was acceptable as we did a walk and talk when he was leaving the building. I also used LIQU Go for liquidations and ultimately settled on LAND Go, I thought that was as generic as possible.

When I began the pilot I thought the staff at SBA were interested in the progress. I was overestimating their interest by a long shot. Ironically when this relationship became adversarial during the litigation I was grateful for the fact that I sent these notices since it was harder for them to deny that they were on notice of some of the pitfalls of trying to get the real estate portfolio sold in bulk. In retrospect the whole contractual experience was litigation.

I would also fax the announcements to potential purchasers on the weekend hoping there would be a response when they hit the ground running on Monday. Unfortunately the enthusiasm for this precious commodity was very limited.

As I entered this section of Disney world I met other small business types. I recall one fellow who was a lobbyist for the U.S Federation of Small Business. I explained the pilot program and he explained to me that the Federation was really an effort to sell insurance and other bundled products by offering discounts and amalgamating the individual small businesses as if they were under one roof. Clever work.

# SALES FROM ALIENS

Meanwhile I was busy orienting the SBA to the sales effort. I printed examples of the SBA inventory and a single offering and faxed them to SBA personnel in D.C. I didn't realize that they were really not in a selling mode and certainly not in bulk. I wanted to go through a familiarization process but they were not interested. In addition to the database on the Bloomberg I took it upon myself to set up the database in my Apple computer. It helped to analyze and identify the properties. The old adage about computer data, garbage in, garbage out was accurate. But I tried to scrub it as much as possible. I have to say that one of the benefits of this experience is a friendship I cultivated with a former SBA official named Mitchell F. Stanley. He was there throughout this nightmare of futility. I recall vividly sitting in my small study and entering the data to do an analysis of holding periods, recovery rates and average pricing. I used this data as a basis for arguing for improvement, but it basically fell on deaf ears.

In April of 1994 I traveled to DC to preview meetings at and with the SBA. In an effort to coordinate contacts with particular properties I started to log that information as well. Regrettably I was slicing and dicing but no one at SBA cared to know my analysis, but the buyers did. I met with Jane Butler at the DC offices of Bloomberg to give her a demonstration. I think she finally grasped the possibilities but when your mind is shut, all the demonstrations on the world won't help very much. It is always a learning experience to see a government official outside of their office in order to accomplish your goals. I also gave a demonstration to Ron Matzner, Associate Deputy General Counsel of the SBA. Ironically, I went to high school with Ron and his wife. They were sympathetic, but I informed people at SBA of the fact that Ron and I knew each other so it was unethical for him to try to influence the proceedings. I would always try to meet with Erskine B. Bowles when I was in the SBA building and usually succeeded. He was always accessible and supportive. That is what carried me through. As I have said, once he was going over to the White House, I knew life would be different, but I didn't realize how tough it would be.

I arranged the first payment from the SBA via fax approval of Jane Butler who was en route to New Orleans. Billy Jenkins was cooperative once approvals were received. Since there weren't too many precedents for pilot programs, I found that being creative for administering the contract was the only approach. They were basically indifferent to the whole project so as long as there were no waves, everything moved forward.

# White House Conference on Small Business

I also would meet with Nick Friendly of the White House Conference on Small Business to discuss regional meetings. In those days, I believed I was part of the Administration's small business initiatives and Nick was a good sounding board. Essentially they were busy organizing a giant small business convention. It impressed me as a junior high school atmosphere once the event started, but I was an appointed delegate and I felt I should participate.

In order to market I would speak with prospective buyers of the Colpur portfolio. I arranged a printout of the entire portfolio, which was a combination of the Bloomberg printouts and my own database report. The scrubbing involved was severe, but as they say when you've got lemons make lemonade.

# Selling Never Stops

As the program went on I used every opportunity to make buyers aware that this distressed real estate portfolio was for sale. I had a wide cross section of buyers. For example, I have friends working at hedge funds, which have since become more visible since the Long Term Capital Growth debacle. Alex Greenberg is a fellow working for Mike Steinhardt, one of the legendary hedge fund managers. Alex introduced me to the in house opportunity, vulture fund person. He was a former Salomon Brothers employee and he seemed interested. It was enormously helpful to be able to show the buyers samples of the portfolio on the Bloomberg. It gave the marketing credibility.

I remember the sense of accomplishment of seeing the database on the Bloomberg. In those days, the Internet was still a research and academic medium, not commercial, so having the portfolio on the Bloomberg was a step forward. To this day people ask me why don't I put the portfolio on the Internet. My answer is simple, you don't know who you are reaching on the Internet, whereas you prequalify people based on their access to the Bloomberg. The Bloomberg audience is upscale, wealthy and is spread throughout the investment community worldwide, banks, insurance companies, brokerage firms, portfolio managers, hedge funds, pension funds, and the press, just to name a few.

# SCAVENGER HUNT

The process of identifying the universe of buyers for distressed real estate in bulk with such small average value was like a scavenger hunt. I was trying to find scavengers using their techniques. As the late Robin O. Clay once said to me, you make your money in shit and spend it in gold. His colleagues couldn't stand the fact that I would make real money. The contract allowed for a 2% to 4% commission and I would refund the $50,000 retainer from those commissions. The emulators are so twisted that they expect people to work for them as a kind of public service. I wake up everyday thinking of the venality of the cabal of the Office of Borrower and Lender Servicing and their protector in the Office of Litigation, Eric S. Benderson. Last night as I was reading Civil Action I was reminded of how apt my description of this cabal as the lagoon was. There was a phrase about the lagoon of arsenic discovered in Woburn, Massachusetts. The lagoon at the SBA is no less poisonous. These senior career officials have made a mockery of what supporting small business is all about. Their arbitrary actions go unnoticed and the people that happen to see the damage and waste that the SBA creates usually condone the behavior to avoid reprisals. As my colleague once told me, the SBA is a pile of rags waiting for a match.

# MY FATHER'S MEMORY

I have achieved a slight nirvana in knowing that I can express my views and hope that they get published and have an impact on the cabal from the lagoon. Litigation is an endless process with an uncertain outcome. Although I am a principled person I am not prepared for penury. The lawyer in Civil Action, Jon Schlichtman wasn't prepared either, but he got there. When I decided to accept the settlement offer from the SBA which was far below the reasonable value of my claim, I reached out to my father's spirit. He passed away on May 26, 1997 and I was devastated by his death. In fact I have still not come to grips with it and don't expect I ever will. His spirit told me something was better than nothing. Nevertheless, the pile of rags must be ignited. Of course these are figures of speech and I don't advocate violence although the concept tempts me sometimes. Fortunately you don't have to murder someone who commits suicide. The liquidation cabal, also known as the emulators will commit organizational suicide. Now that they are selling 10 billion in assets the chicanery and venality will come to light and they will have no alternative but to take their own lives by resigning.

# Undetected Cancer

I have been exposed to a wide variety of people in my travels but the cabal at the SBA are like a cancer that remains undetected and then radiation is used in desperation. In this case I am persuaded that they will be their own undoing, but I will nudge them as much as I can. It scares me that I may sound like a mild form of Mein Kampf, however I have a pact with myself to see these amateurs get their due.

# PROSPECTING

One prospect was Frank Healy of Ocwen in Florida. The name was scientifically created by spelling New Company backward with company abbreviated. This was a referral from Jerry Silver, a mortgage finance independent broker from East Hampton who I found through a grammar school friend from California. This is the search method based on the concept that there are 40 people in the whole world and I know all of them. I met with Jerry Silver and walked him through the portfolio and after that it drifted into no interest from Ocwen or Silver.

I discussed the pilot program with just about everyone I spoke with from the business, political or social world in the hope that someone would emerge. One buyer worked for a merchant bank that was formed a few years ago by Bankers Trust executives that had offices worldwide. He contacted me about a foreclosure on the Bloomberg and then I would break into my Colpur routine if I sensed it was an institutional rather than an individual buyer.

# Colson Culprits

---

Colson Services Corporation occupies a special place in the SBA universe. They organize the secondary market loans that comprise the securities that trade in the public markets. I contacted this SBA servicer as to the nature of their responsibility and how they might assist information gathering for COLPUR. They were not very helpful. I didn't fit into the existing structure of their relationship so I was meaningless to them.

In the spring of 1994 I had authorization to begin the pilot program. Alex Greenberg came over to Bloomberg's offices in New York and I did a demo of the database of foreclosures. The database was numerically coded and I knew the range of property ID#s for SBA was 89719 to 90175. The RTC range was 113266 to 118950. I was able to differentiate between the portfolios using the numbered Ids. It is important to realize the unscrubbed nature of the data, so any means of making order out of the chaos was a plus.

I had to consider my own financial position in order to maintain the pilot program on the limited budget and I spoke with an accountant to finalize documentation for a SBA loan to improve my financial position in contemplation of the pilot program. The

SBA doesn't provide loans eagerly and I didn't have any collateral so my prospects were dim for financing. They say the best time to borrow is when you don't need the money.

# REVERSE CHARM SCHOOL

Some of the people I dealt with at SBA were pleasant. Ironically the further away you were from DC, the kinder the individuals were. For example when I had to deal with payment problems I would confirm payment with Rory Berges and Elmer Dean of the SBA regional office in Colorado. They were always polite and helpful.

# Watch Your Flanks

I frequently spoke with John Loza to arrange the page feature to enable buyers to scroll through the portfolio on the Bloomberg. He was a programmer at Bloomberg who was generally helpful. Nevertheless he gave me a mini coronary when he decided to give the FORE access to an outsider from Nomura Securities without telling me or getting clearance from anyone. I always had to watch my flanks and the moment I heard about this mistake I called Elizabeth DeMarse who was one of Michael Bloomberg's top aides. Luckily she knew Michael was staying with a former Salomon colleague over the weekend in East Hampton. So I tracked him down and the problem went away rapidly. I didn't need the extra headache of losing my access to the Bloomberg by a renegade programmer.

# PERMANENT CAMPAIGN

As I write this saga I look inside myself to understand the motivation. It came to me while reading about President Clinton's battles with Kenneth Starr. It was characterized as the permanent campaign. Now I've got it. This will be part of my permanent campaign. Similar to the advice in City Slickers by Curly, in a man's life there is one thing and when you know that one thing, it gives your life direction and meaning. So consider yourself part of my permanent campaign as you read this story.

# MICROSOFT VERSUS APPLE

In the beginning of the pilot program I kept slicing and dicing the portfolio. I was still relying on the Appleworks software and I entered in the data describing the properties and tried to get some consistency or categories. I was not proficient in Microsoft compatible software and I would have saved a lot of time if I had a better understanding of using the Microsoft database programs. It took me years to convert my thinking and make use of the database using Microsoft. So in an effort to market I printed out a database of the Colpur real estate after I entered it into a separate database to sort and locate.

In retrospect I could have collected my funds and filed reports and there would have been little opposition. The SBA's constant mantra was you haven't sold anything yet, to which I would respond you haven't given me close to the amount of information I need to get serious interest in the portfolio. In one of my favorite observations, Arnold S. Rosenthal, a senior member of the Office of Borrower and Lender Services suggested I should try to sell the properties that they had so graciously given me the photos and minimal property descriptions. The idiocy of that position showed how little market savvy these staff people had. Privatization becomes more appealing after you work with the 3-D staffers, delay, derail, and defer but rarely decide.

# Moving the Trash

In the spirit of all that goes around comes around. There will come a day in this saga that the retrospective will coincide with the steps I took 5 years ago to move the trash as Erskine B. Bowles once told me. When I first met him in May 1993 he told me that there was a saying in the South that when someone is considered an effective person they say that he can move the trash. I always used that line when I tried to keep Erskine informed on my progress.

I was introduced to a mortgage broker in East Hampton, N.Y. by a childhood friend of mine who lives in California. This broker had a relationship with a group called Ocwen which is New Company abbreviated and spelled backwards. I printed out the Colpur Portfolio and delivered the list to a prospective purchaser Ocwen of Florida. I should have realized the omen that occurred when I left his street and a small rock created a crack in my windshield. Somehow small obstacles never stopped me.

# Buzz Phrases

In order to have some buzz phrases to describe the portfolio I tried numerical analysis.

I analyzed the data and determined the average cost of the Colpur was $367,529.63. That meant there were properties worth as much as a million dollars, but there were also properties worth very little. The deterioration of an abandoned property is substantial. One of my favorites was the warehouse in Brooklyn. I took the subway to view the property and as I got closer I realized I was entering unfriendly territory. I actually befriended 2 burly brothers who were bouncers in Greenwich Village in case I ran into any interference on the subway. The first time I visited the property I noticed that the front door wasn't locked. There are supposed to be caretakers for the building when it is foreclosed and held by the SBA, but I guess they didn't bother to lock up. Not surprisingly, the next time I came to see the property, the locals decided to have a small bonfire in the building. This is not exactly an enhancement to the value.

# GARBAGE IN GARBAGE OUT

In order to get fresh information I contacted the assigned SBA personnel for particular COLPUR properties. They were somewhat helpful. Frequently the information was stale, but I was able to find out about other properties that were available. For the most part, there was little awareness that I had the contract and not much interest. One of my memorable encounters was after the 1994 pilot program. I had a meeting with the New York Regional Director, Thomas Bettridge, and the Counsel, Celeste Kaptur. She had the appeal of a machine gun and the same delivery. When I was trying to explain that even the RTC allowed for broker participation in the sales, she was like an attack dog, barking all the possible obstacles and displayed such hostility that when she left the room Tom Bettridge and I looked at each other with a look of total incredulity. How could any reasonable person behave in such a manner? Looking back, she was obviously trained in the Eric Benderson-Gary Fox School of Law. Essentially they take the most extreme views and remain inflexible. So when I described my marketing efforts in the annual written report Gary Fox would say that I could have put everyone listed in the telephone book and then claim they were prospective purchasers. The only problem wit that extreme position is that I didn't do that and I tried to target the prospects to purchasers that might have some interest in the foreclosures. It is disturbing that the quality of the legal representation at the SBA is so over the top. They were rude and irrational, but other than that I couldn't wait to discuss issues with them. Gary Fox probably had a sales job and went through the phone book that way. I'm sure he tried to enhance his social life that way. He has all of Ken Starr's charm and none of his looks.

# APPLES AND ORANGES

I was able to sort the data using the database I had entered into my Apple computer. It took me years to have the necessary command of the Microsoft database programs. It made matters worse that Microsoft created the Windows 95 system. This was an upgrade from the Microsoft Works system. It took me years to understand the distinction and have the ability to open files that I created under one system or the other. Fortunately the Apple system was easy for me to use once I completed entering the data. I was able to sort by State and property type and give purchasers a better handle on what was in the portfolio. I also created a database of SBA personnel in Florida, California, N.Y., Alabama and Arizona. I faxed information about the pilot program as an introduction but it didn't have much of an impact.

# THE LUDSIN MODEL

---

This proposal will provide for a managed competitive format to dispose of the surplus assets of the Small Business Administration as well as other government agencies. Essentially it is composed of two elements, the appraisal function and the disposition function.

The appraisal function will be conducted by a private independent entity using independent fee appraisers to evaluate the assets. The cost of that evaluation will be borne by the investors. The projected cost is 2% of the asking price of the assets. The funds will be placed in a separate account and the losing bidders will receive a refund of their expenditure plus interest. The winning bidder's refund will be a deposit towards the purchase price. The refund will come from the commission earned by the disposition agent.

The commission to the disposition agent will be 4% of the sales price. The 2% appraisal fee will come out of the 4% commission. Thus the bidders will provide the first phase of the financing of the appraisal. The disposition agent will receive a 2% commission which has been industry wide practice.

In keeping with the zigzag recounting of this story, it appears that the SBA has adopted the "Ludsin Model". They are requiring a $20,000 deposit in order to review the loan documents. I had advocated a larger refundable deposit to cover the costs of the appraisals. I wonder how many investors would be willing to put up the funds.

# Momentum Killers

The key to progress in the pilot program was momentum. I genuinely believed that there was a buyer out there, particularly after the RTC and the S & L bailout. I realized this was a very optimistic view but I had to be a dreamer in order to get the job done. I was still energized enough to go to DC to discuss the pilot program and get more cooperation, but it is safe to say that basically I was tolerated and mildly entertaining to the senior career officials who really had minimal interest in changing the way they were doing business. Their familiarity with Wall Street or the Bloomberg was superficial at best. I assumed the pilot would be extended so I didn't press too hard during the first six months in an effort to get the career officials used to my existence. I knew things would change when I visited Erskine B. Bowles in September 1994 and he was wrapping up his days as SBA Administrator to become deputy chief of staff in the White House. His replacement was Philip Lader, a wooden sort of fellow who had all the right moves, but I am still befuddled as to how much substance he has. He is now the Ambassador to Great Britain, which is a true example of the Peter Principle. He rose to his level of incompetence, but then again the job requirements may be well suited for the pomp and ceremony without any critical decisions required. It hurts to think I had come in such close proximity with these political appointees, but was left to fend for myself with the senior career officials. These career officials sole reason for being appears to be to keep the trains running and they don't even have a schedule to worry about.

# SENSE OF HUMOR

While I was pursuing the pilot program, the White House Conference on Small Business was beginning its roadshow. The first outreach was in Wilmington, Delaware. It was poetic that I as I arrived, Alan Patricof was leaving. Alan was the head of the WHCSB and an accomplished venture capitalist. Humor isn't a strong suit for him, but he generally cordial. Early in the days of Erskine's becoming Administrator I ran into Alan Patricof in the SBA Headquarters in Washington, D.C. He turned to me and asked, What are you doing here? To which I responded, The same thing you are. He then quickly responded saying no you're not. I responded saying just kidding. In any event Alan had been a major Clinton fundraiser and being Chairman of the White House Conference on Small Business was the payback. I had tried to leverage my appointment as the Congressional Delegate from Manhattan to give further credibility to the pilot program. Ironically it helped me get elected as Chairman of the downstate delegation from New York. I never had the opportunity to assume my duties because all my energies were devoted to getting the contract renewed. It took me from October 1994 to June 12, 1995, the opening day of the White House Conference on Small Business in Washington, D.C. Life is timing.

# Old Executive Office Building

I am a believer in killing two birds with one stone. I felt that the pilot program was a small part of the reinvention of government initiatives so I tried to keep the Gore folks informed. I met with Greg Simons on the Vice President's staff and he was supportive. I also kept contacts with the newly created National Economic Council. Tom Kalil actually gave us a chance to present the concept of computer marketing of government assets. I remember there was a severe ice storm and he said he was still available to meet. So I marched in with Mitchell F. Stanley, a former Deputy Administrator of the SBA and a dear friend, and Matthew R. Schneider, an attorney in DC who I went to Cornell with. It was a constructive meeting and Tom actually drew the concept on the blackboard and I was proud that I was a part of policy even though the blackboard was erased shortly thereafter. I maintained contacts with the Office of Public Liaison since they had created a subdivision for small business, which was the thrust of my concept of the Office of Small Business Liaison. I recall seeing a memo during the pilot program in 1994 with a list of small business interagency names. I contacted most of those folks and for a time I kept them informed about the pilot program. In retrospect

I probably wasn't the front burner item on the their agenda, but I had fun believing I was part of their grand scheme.

# HOLE IN THE ROOF

One of my favorite road trips was to Syracuse, N.Y., followed by a visit to Oswego, N.Y. to visit my first piece of Colpur, the Oswego Boiler plant. I expect the photograph of that property will be in this book. Oswego had a deserted quality, kind of like a freeze frame. You could see Theodore Dreiser characters in the ghosts of this giant boiler plant. I met a kindly gentleman who had the keys. He was the town manager and he walked me inside, warning that I should be careful since the roof had collapsed. I thought the location was ideal, on the land along the locks which were being gentrified. There was a home for the elderly next door. Unfortunately, no one else shared my vision. I found out there was a group building a museum for the lucky souls who survived the Holocaust and were transplanted in Oswego by the Roosevelt administration. I thought this site would work as a museum site, but they were going to use property on a nearby military base.

# AFTERMATH

---

At the risk of confusing the sequence, I want to share my recent experience with the 7 contractors eligible to do due diligence. I was able to reach 6 out of the seven. They have already created the teams of subcontractors when they responded to the RFP (Request for Proposal). I thought I would dazzle them with the video of the Colpur that I have been able to create with a new graphics card and software. I have come to the conclusion that any new business concept takes a year until people get used to having you in the loop and willing to share information with you.

Back to June 1994, I contacted the SBA district offices regarding the Colpur pilot program. I received materials from Donald Procop of the Syracuse Office regarding the Oswego Boiler Corp. and the environmental problems associated with that property. I was encouraged that I got a response and given what I know now, that was a minor miracle. The SBA offices are sleepy affairs, not known for their output.

# NEW YORK, NEW YORK

I also tried to stay close to home. I met with Tom Bettridge, Regional Director of the NY SBA office to discuss the pilot program and possible financing. He was a decent fellow and had an interesting background, having done some work in Bedford Stuyvesant, a poverty section in Brooklyn. I also noticed photos of racing motorcycles, apparently that was Tom's hobby. He was supportive of my efforts and he made me think that my efforts would be met with cooperation. I have since discovered that the appointees are viewed by the staff like guests who they pray will leave soon enough so that the career staff can go back to business as usual.

# ALICE IN WONDERLAND

I was a like Alice in Wonderland discovering these programs that I thought would be helpful but were more in the order of propaganda than actual help. When you deal with small business support it reminds of the saying that the time to borrow is when you don't need the money. There was an educational outreach from Pace University in New York trying to help small business. These programs get federal funds and try to point small business people in the right direction. After a few meetings and phone conversations I realized the likelihood of funding for the pilot program and the computer marketing concept was slim.

# CAVE DWELLER

The concept of the cave dweller came to me after watching a documentary about the Clinton's and their rise to power. The resistance to their new ideas was prevalent amongst the permanent Washington power circles who exist regardless of who is President. It reminded me of the fierce resistance I experienced in my quest to sell assets for the SBA. It is apparent that the value of my experience is better described as a how-to approach. How can an individual try to achieve a goal when there are roadblocks and obstacles that are pre-existing or constructed by the cave dwellers to assure your ultimate failure or demise? I took the approach that was similar to investigative journalism but I wasn't trying to expose the career officials, I was trying to get them to cooperate with me. The saying goes, When charm fails, use the hammer. Accordingly, I tried valiantly to relate to the managers in the Office of Borrower and Lender Servicing, but I wasn't one of them.

How do you become one of them? The answer is you don't, because you can't. But you have to try.

The simultaneous job of finding buyers and keeping the seller massaged was demanding. They say the sign of a genius is someone who can have two opposite ideas in their mind at the same time and not crack up. Thus, when you find yourself in a squeeze, allow yourself the room to have the conflicting ideas flourish together. In other words, it is one thing just to get the buyer to step up to the plate. It is quite another to bring a recalcitrant, or in this case a non-existent seller, to the table. Yet you can't get discouraged because after a while they get used to the idea that the assets are in play. One way to keep the information flow going is to visit with a wide group from both sides.

In June 8 1994 I displayed the Colpur portfolio to Steinhardt Partners at offices of Bloomberg. This is a well-known hedge fund. The ability to showcase the portfolio at Bloomberg enhanced the marketing effort and gave the project more credibility. The ability to pull up the information and images quickly on the screen gets people's attention and you have the opportunity to present your wares wherever you can locate a Bloomberg.

I also traveled to upstate New York and met with Donald Procop and Ken Jackson in Syracuse SBA office to discuss the pilot program and view the Oswego Package Boiler Company factory. As I discussed above, it was a total relic and felt like going back on time. I had a sense of mission then and it opened my eyes to the simple fact that there was a large portfolio of non performing properties just sitting there waiting to be plucked.

# It's A Family Affair

All that goes around comes around. It turns out that the due diligence for the first 350 million dollar sale of the 7(a) loans is being done with a partner of Rick Hernandez, the counselor to the Administrator, Erskine B. Bowles. Small world. The fellow from that due diligence firm mentioned concerns about contacting the field offices. I told him he had his work cut out for him.

# CORNELL SPIRIT

I was trying to use a variety of methods just to get the word out. I visited Cornell University for a reunion weekend in 1994. I discussed the pilot program at Cornell University Business School with a view to increase awareness and set up an MBA case study. I tried to find an interested professor but it didn't really grab them. I was pleased to see there was a Bloomberg in the library. It is always reassuring to see something familiar when you're traveling, especially when it is a sophisticated information system you are relying on to sell your wares. After I entered the database into the Apple computer I printed and mailed a 31 page printout summarizing the Colpur portfolio for potential purchasers. Since real estate is like politics, local, local, local I tried to interest investors in New York City to consider the properties in upstate New York. I sent information about the Oswego Boiler Plant in Oswego N.Y. to prospective purchasers. Somehow I felt that an old building on valuable property might be appealing to a turnaround investor.

# SCORE US 0, THEM 0

Occasionally examples of the backward thinking at SBA appear in the media and it behooves me to tell you about it. In any quest to deal with an impenetrable organization one must keep a dossier on the shortcomings. The New York Times had a piece about Retired Executives Offer Help on Line. I couldn't help but be struck by the counterintuitive consulting by the SCORE staff at the SBA. It is particularly irksome that there are substantial sums in the Federal budget to perpetuate a program that is hopelessly outdated. Doesn't it strike you as odd that retired executives are rejecting Internet marketing ideas while they are simultaneously being tutored on how to use a computer? The retired executives deserve credit for helping but it is disturbing that these counselors are woefully uninformed. Do you really need a retired executive to help you network through email? It is a sad case of propaganda that is supposed to help small business when the reality is that the SCORE executives require basic computer training. Why not admit that they are better qualified to deal with traditional business creation issues like capital formation or accounting and stay away from topics that they aren't qualified to dispense knowledge about? Small business creators would be better served spending their time elsewhere and Congress should take a hard look as to whether they are getting any meaningful value for the SCORE program appropriations. Instead more money is spent to educate anachronisms. It is inexcusable that SCORE staff are ignorant of basic computer usage and they are holding themselves out as consultants. It's the blind leading the seers. The SCORE is retired executives 5 and small business 0.

# Yme2?

Yme2? That is the theme of an Op Ed piece that stems directly from the experience with Washington. Internet marketing is touted as the equivalent of the industrial revolution. I was the skunk at the picnic when I tried to sell Washington on the idea of marketing on the information highway known as Bloomberg. Now I'm the skunk again by alerting the boosters of Internet marketing that there is a missing link. Personal contact doesn't happen with vivid graphics and profit doesn't come from advertising that hasn't been sold.

# Marvin Gardens

---

February 26 1999 deja vu in Florida 2 years ago I was excitedly calling Chase Magnuson the first bulk bidder in 1997. I also recall Marvin Gardens in Vero Beach. I recall the meeting with Lader, Spotilla and the crew to demonstrate the pictures and appraisal info on the laptop through the Bloomberg; it was set up to self-destruct as far as they were concerned. I also recall the 2 Coral Gables office visits. The first one was after the pilot program. I was kept waiting for 45 minutes and there was little to talk about. The second time I had the contract so they presented their crew and placated me for a half-hour or so. I recall the son of the German ambassador to Cuba, during the Nazi era was the part of the SBA staff, which made very uneasy.

I think about the smugness and imperturbability of the SBA staff and I am reminded that the laws and regs keep them well insulated. That insulation will work against them during the exposure of the back end of their operations. There is very little follow up and some of the loose ends will come back to haunt them.

The second anniversary of the first bulk bid with letter of intent occurred when I was in Florida. It is a bittersweet memory particularly because my father was still alive when I was trying to get the deal done. After he died I tried to remain strong but it was trying.

Perseverance counts, I received a call from a small biz lender about vacant land in Camden. I am always gratified when someone remembers my pitch for business. Unfortunately many of the foreclosures were truly distressed so it took a patient and skilled investor to be willing to take the risk.

By March of 1999 the experience was behind me but the scars weren't. I was in Florida and it had a special resonance because for a brief period it appeared that I might succeed once the first bid came in. I also remember having the chance to see my father when he was still healthy. Unfortunately by May 1999 he passed away and my life hasn't been the same since. In fact I dedicate this book to his memory because it was his optimism and belief in me that inspires to complete this story.

I should add that I am a film buff and I spent many hours avoiding depression or being discouraged by watching Shawshank Redemption. At the end of the story of a bank executive wrongfully convicted of his wife's murder, he delivers a package to the local newspaper exposing the corruption in the prison. It was that insider's story that brought down the warden and his staff. I don't believe the political appointees can change the environment at the SBA because it is so ingrained, but you have to try. It is now July 4, 2000 and I read excerpts of an interview in the New York Times about the definition of patriotism. Victor Navasky said it was about striving for the American ideal s and improving the society. That is also a motivation for me. I believe the Government agencies could do better if someone took the time to monitor their activities or lack thereof.

Right now the SBA atmosphere is best-described incompetence with inactivity for its own sake with their credo: our way or no way.

After surviving the SBA's brand of lunacy becoming a consultant is the logical conclusion assuming logic applies. It is an unusual phenomenon that people expect you to work for free until a deal is done. The risk is assigned to the person or company least able to accept it. In Washington there is a level of prestige to working on federal matters, but the days of the dollar a year man are numbered. People with old wealth can serve in that capacity, but most people can't.

The second anniversary of my FOIA oral argument in the Second Circuit also occurred when I was in Florida. That was a shining moment. I trained as litigator but I found the practice of law too arduous for my skills. Nevertheless, I totally rehearsed my oral argument as to why the SBA was acting arbitrarily when they invoked the $10,250 processing fee. At the end of my presentation the presiding judge of the three-judge Appeals Panel said I was at the top of the list. I looked up at him with a puzzled look and he expanded his comments. He said I was at the top of the list of attorneys appearing on their own behalf and that I made an excellent presentation. I was proud of that moment. I also sensed that my father's spirit was with me at that oral argument. I wished he could have seen it, but I know he was proud.

Themes along the way emerged. Be careful what you want you might get it. That was the blind side I hadn't thought through. I was so optimistic that I didn't have an exit strategy. My prior experience with the RTC should have alerted me, but after getting the enormous head of steam that I had when President Clinton was elected, I assumed there would be just rewards. The only reward was the lesson to not try to make money in Washington; they're there to take your money. I also reminded myself of the movie Jerry Maguire and his client's mantra: Show me the money.

Burn Rate by Michael Wolff was also inspiring. He wrote about his quest to finance an Internet TV Guide publication. It is reassuring that were other dreamers who saw the possibilities of the information highway but didn't have all their ducks in a row.

When I think about the problems of Internet marketing one clear issue is the source of revenues: advertising revenues or transactions? The growth of this phenomenon is similar to the advent of television in the fifties. There were many skeptics and their cynicism was overrun by the public's need to be informed and entertained. It's like going to the library in your pajamas. For sales people it saves cold calling. It shifts the ball, because after seeing a website, the ball is in your court. Internet marketing is important because of what we don't know. Information alone isn't marketing.

# YME2? OP-ED

This is an Op-Ed piece I submitted to the New York Times which wasn't published but it raises many of the issues I encountered when I tried to use the commercial opportunities presented by the new technology.

Internet marketing is touted as the equivalent of the industrial revolution. I was the skunk at the picnic when I tried to sell Washington on the idea of marketing government assets on the information highway known as Bloomberg. It could have been any Intranet, like Reuters or Bridge. Many people asked me why I didn't put the assets for sale on the Internet also. I responded that a private Intranet helped me focus who the buyers are and I didn't want to be overwhelmed with tire kickers and people who were "just looking". Now I'm the skunk again by alerting the boosters of Internet marketing that there is a missing link. Personal contact doesn't happen with vivid graphics and profit doesn't come from advertising that hasn't been sold or merchandise that is sold slowly, if at all.

# GENESIS

How I got here requires a brief historical background. I started with Apple computers in 1984 and shifted to Microsoft compatible computers in 1995, which was no small feat. In September 1989, I approached the RTC to sell their real estate on the information highway. By the time they seriously considered the concept, the RTC evaporated and became part of the FDIC. I believed the Clinton Administration's policy of helping small business, reinventing government and using the information highway so I approached the Small Business Administration, which allegedly assists entrepreneurs. I succeeded in getting a pilot program in 1994 to sell their foreclosed real estate on the information highway and then I had a follow on contract in 1995 to complete the sales. Although I found buyers for a bulk sale of the real estate, the SBA forgot to mention they needed approval from the lenders to sell the properties.

The late philosopher Isaiah Berlin said that humanity is split between hedgehogs and foxes. Hedgehogs believe in one overall principle and then approach life through that prism. Foxes see events from many perspectives and adjust according to the changes that are inevitable in human events. It should come as no surprise that the Government as a seller is the hedgehog, inflexible and prone to obfuscation. But fortunately marketing on the Internet involves the sale of goods from the private sector.

You have to avoid being road kill on the information highway. Be careful what you want you might get it. In his book <u>Burn Rate</u>, Michael Wolff told an entertaining saga of his efforts to raise capital for an Internet TV Guide publication. It was evident that no one really knew what to expect from this medium. I am reminded of the theme of the movie Jerry Maguire, "show me the money". What is the source of revenues for Internet marketing: advertising revenues to the providers and search engines and transactions for the sellers. The growth of the Internet as a commercial pipeline is similar to the advent of television in the fifties. Some skeptics doubted it would catch on but ultimately the possibilities multiplied.

It is like going to the library in your pajamas when you sign on with your computer. As a child I remember a mixture of dread and anticipation when I had to research a problem in the library. Going through the infinite file card system and then following the Dewey decimal system were hurdles. Now your search has ended. Just enter the keyword and you are at least half way there, saving countless hours and disappointment.

Using the same ease of execution to sell will make our lives easier and efficient, but vendor beware. The follow up to prospector's calls is to look at the website. In traditional sales you usually see the client at least once. A camera on the monitor helps and you can get the immediate attention through email, but web sites are like billboards on the highway. For sellers, Internet marketing saves cold calling and prospecting. It shifts the ball into the buyers' court because the presentation is there all the time just by typing in some access letters. But there still is no substitute for human interaction. That's why Mary Kay or the Fuller Brush man existed. Of course Willy Lomans existed too. So maybe we are making the loneliness and repeated rejection of the door to door salesman a thing of the past, but every sale requires someone to close, and a lasting business requires profit.

I recently attended an Information Technology exposition at the Javits Center in New York. By the time I stopped at the third booth I couldn't help but read a promotional brochure stating that you can achieve "personal contact through rich visual imagery". To me that said it all, and that is the fallacy of Internet marketing. There is no substitute for actually meeting a buyer or investor. It reminds me of Roosevelt's fireside chats on the radio giving the illusion of being in your home and providing comforting words to the information hungry populace. Now you peddle your wares instantly and remain on someone's radar screen, but for how long if at all?

Internet marketing is important because of what we don't know. Information alone isn't marketing. It is true that you can get someone's attention. You can buy and sell securities and save yourself a trip to the mall by buying from the electronic catalogs. Nevertheless, there is a danger that increasing isolation will lead to diminished needs. In other words once you have filled your home or office with the necessary creature comforts you won't be induced to increase your purchases. You won't be privy to the pitches of the sales staff in the department stores encouraging you to sample the perfume or taste the dip.

Virtual reality isn't reality. The Internet is deconstructing the society, in some ways telecommuting us back to the cave. Using the information highway as the medium for sales propaganda is the retailers' dream, but it isn't going to come out the way we planned it.

The jury is still out on just how high the upside is. It doesn't mean we should suspend sales on the Internet until we solve the enigma of unlimited exposure of a product, but questionable receptivity and final sales. Just be careful before you give up your day job.

# LENDER CONSENT

Even as late as March 3 1999 the issue of lender consent arises again for the TFA (Transaction Financial Advisor) on the first sale now wonders about Benderson's raising this issue. It is pathetic that the SBA put me through all that effort knowing they could not sell. I believe the lenders would have listened to the SBA and allowed a bulk sale, but the lagoon wanted to stay in the dark ages. They're more comfortable in the dark, like roaches that don't scatter until someone turns the lights on. Now the SBA found new victims in the form of the new contractors.

By March 1999 the SBA budget increased by 17 percent to 995 million, just shy of the one billion-dollar threshold when Washington might think about focusing on the agency's activities. The prospect of throwing more funds more such administrative incompetence is revolting.

I tried to make inroads with the other private sector contractors including an outfit called Colson Services. They were simply a regional office of stonewallers trained by the masters from the lagoon. I had a meeting with them in their old offices which were a credit to the cause of low overhead. I explained that it would be helpful to know more about the collateral of loans that went into default and that they should feel free to keep me posted. It was like attending an admissions committee hearing when you knew there was a slim chance you would be accepted. They nodded assent, looked at each other with blank stares and then went back to business as usual. Men in black suits with little to distinguish them except an exclusive contract to manage the loan pools of small business loans guaranteed by the SBA. They were narrow in terms of their focus.

I kept on believing that 5 years of work had to have value. Apart from avoiding any business relationship with the Federal government, and writing this book, I have become a dotcom consultant helping other ecommerce companies to raise funds and avoid pitfalls. I needed to create value added through reliving the nightmarish history of the pilot program and the contract to do electronic marketing.

The propaganda from the Administrator keeps flowing to the Senate Small Business Committee. The SBA has a symbiotic relationship with the oversight committees. Once in a while the SBA does something that is even shocking to the members of the House or Senate Small Business Committees and so they hold a hearing. There are seats for about 50 people on the Senate side and more on the House side. After going through the motions and making critical statements, reports are filed and then everyone waits for the next act. Always business as usual with the occasional moments of drama, but mostly it's don't rock the boat.

Meanwhile the better battleground to keep the lagoon oxygenated is the press and I revived the communication to the Thrift Liquidation Alert, now known as Real Estate Alert. TLA is the acronym. It is a solid industry report. I met with a delightful reporter named David Levitt. I tried to explain to him that there was a lot of questionable conduct at the SBA. But he wasn't looking for the Pulitzer Prize and if he was, it wouldn't have been a story about the lagoon. Nevertheless, he was thorough and did a good job of covering the SBA asset sales that began in 1999.

The SBA's program of modernization was really a euphemism for liquidation of the back end of their loan programs. Now that I look back on it, they were masters as using profound sounding phrases to describe damage control. Most of the time they react, they don't initiate. Remember anything below a billion in Washington doesn't matter, and the idlers are left to their own devices. Oversight is really kabuki theater; they go through the motions out of tradition, but very little happens in the way of change.

At times I thought of myself as a wildcatter I kept drilling for information in this deep hole which has taken on the characteristics of an onion, layered and smelly. As I write this saga, I am reminded of the artist in his studio with the unfinished canvas staring him in the face. The contract implementation had he same quality and as you can tell I tried to give it my all. Nevertheless if the SBA didn't want you to succeed all they had to do is business as usual and soon the victim would either give up or die. I coined the word econocide to describe the process, they have no hesitation to kill you economically, in fact they like the spectacle. Watching the movie Gladiator brought back that feeling of defiance against crude people in positions of power, but how do I feel about them?

Along the way, I thought some press exposure of the lagoon would be constructive but generally it was a tough sale. At one point I went to 60 Minutes and ran into Don Hewitt, the senior Producer and quickly told him my story at the time I was trying to get the appraisals. His response was friendly but he characterized as a "$10,000" story. I couldn't get him to understand it was really a $100 million story. It just wasn't very sexy. Bumbling bureaucrats are nothing new; perhaps if I filmed the cast of characters the press would have jumped on the story. You couldn't find better specimens in central casting or a human laboratory for Darwin's evolution, early stages of man that is.

By Spring of '99 I tried to make some money as a consultant to investors for the first large loan sale conducted by SBA. I soon discovered most investors like to pay a success fee, i.e., if they succeed in buying the portfolio then you get paid. At some point you realize you're working for nothing and it loses it's appeal. Nevertheless I tried to gather information so I sent due diligence inquiries to Metec KPMG SBA, which was a subcontractor arrangement where a minority owned firm affiliates with a major contractor and they get beneficial treatment in the procurement process. Rick Hernandez, former counselor to the SBA Administrator ended up at this firm but he wasn't responding. I became an outsider and radioactive after I tried to actually get something accomplished.

# CONTRACTOR INSULATION

The pattern continues. SBA hires contractors and then discovers they can't deliver the goods. The contractors get paid and the assets are sold in the old fashioned way, if at all.

# Apathy at the Back End

At one point I was moved to file a FOIA request to find out the names of contractors of the SBA. I placed a call to my trusted contact David Fishman who ended up being my lawyer entry point. Well guess what? They didn't keep such a list. What a surprise. I'm pretty sure there was a list, but remember their first reaction is don't know or not sure and they hope you'll move on.

The long road to the marketplace never ends. When I look back I realize that the $50 to $100 million of real estate was a drop in the lake of the federal budget not the bucket. As one person put it more poetically, it was a pimple on the ass of an elephant. After all the SBA has a 994 million-dollar budget. At times I believed there was a conscious decision to delay to give SBA employees a chance to retire and take advantage of privatization. They knew more about the assets and loans than anyone did and after a while even they might develop champagne tastes or should I say wine coolers?

After surviving the SBA I consider myself an expert on government torpor. It's just a glacial operation that occasionally experiences a landslide or avalanche and then returns to idling and moving at the speed of an ant.

I will never forget the artful dodging by Arnold S. Rosenthal, the poster child of government retardation. When we asked him in a deposition what he deemed a bulk sale he responded that 2 properties would constitute a bulk sale. This was a way to show that my contract was just business as usual when he knew damn well that the concept of electronic marketing was to sell to institutional investors found on the Bloomberg and sell the portfolio in its entirety or 100 properties at a time. For example, California had about 177 properties and the highest bidder, the Carlyle Group, was willing to buy the whole portfolio.

The hidden maze of telephone numbers in SBA is emerging at KPMG and when this sale ends the SBA will choose another contractor who will have to start all over. In other words the asset sales are like Bedouins who set up their tents, sleep in the desert and then move on. By the time you have the situation under control the SBA has another contractor and it's back to ground zero.

Even with the presence of private contractors the train is out of the station but the trip is short and readily subject to derailment. And they wonder why Americans are fed up with government. You have to be very dedicated to work towards improvement.

One of the worst things about dealing with the lagoon was that everything was a zero sum game, you win, they lose. The concept is totally alien to these folks. They can't conceive of a win win. I guess how they got their jobs. It reminds me of the early days of the RTC (the Savings and Loan Bailout Agency). When I first broached the idea of electronic marketing with them I started by calling a fellow named Tom Hamburger. He referred me to Thomas Horton who then referred me to Tommy Thompson. When I finally met Tommy Thompson, I asked him if you had to be named Tom in order to get a job with the RTC. He smiled, but I think humor was clearly not a requirement. I also recall Tommy Thompson's reaction when he tried to fit me into the minority contractor window. He said to me, "Too bad Jews aren't a minority for purposes of the legislation". I looked at him, slightly befuddled and I realized that life had reached new levels of absurdity. I was a charter member of the President's Commission on the Holocaust and the U.S. Holocaust Memorial Council which built the Holocaust Museum in Washington. So here I am thinking how absurd the minority legislation is, because even though one third of the world's Jews were killed, we're not a minority because we're not presumed to be disadvantaged. Please explain this phenomenon to me because after dealing with the Federal government for 10 years with a sound business concept I don't feel especially advantaged. Any doubts I had about that fact were brought home to me by the SBA because mediocrity is king there and any deviation is not only a threat but it is punishable by econocide.

As I reflect on the whole nightmare the phrase lender consent keeps haunting me. That was the poison pill, if all else failed the cabal would invoke this excuse for not doing a bulk sale. Naturally they knew it all along, but the method of econocide is to let your victim twist in the wind until they blow away or die, or both. The cabal figured they could assure the defeat of the initiative by grossly interpreting loan language to their benefit. They were so accomplished at the technique that they believed their own lies so I guess it wouldn't be perjury. In truth, the SBA called the shots with the lenders and the banks since it was the Federal Guarantee the SBA was blessing the banks with. If the loan failed, the U.S. Government through the SBA guaranteed 80% of their losses. So if the SBA wanted to do the bulk sale it is unlikely there would have been any resistance. The banks would go along because as a practical matter they had to.

In the small world category Fred Terrell of CS First Boston, the first bulk bidder in December 1995 was also was on the Certified Development Corporation's advisory board. This is an effort to stimulate the inner cities and economically downtrodden areas with funding programs. He was generally helpful, but in retrospect he wouldn't have defied the SBA too much because he was on one of their advisory boards. In fact all the bidders had to dance to the music of the SBA since they made the rules up as they went along and would act as arbitrarily as possible, just for sport and because they were only able to see one foot in front of their nose.

One of the approved contractors, Kevin McMahon is part of the program financial advisor team. His brilliance was overwhelming with the catchy slogan on his business card: even great ideas need landing gears. You just can't wait to sign him up as part of your team. Of course his bland presence led me to believe he had been hanging around the lagoon long enough to be indispensable to the cabal's decision making, and he started having some of the DNA needed for dithering.

# 20 20 HINDSIGHT

The irony of my 20 20 hindsight is how clear it is now that the deck was stacked all along. There was never going to be the big pay day because that would have been a threat to the mediocrity of the cabal. They could never be that creative or gutsy to move the trash, as Erskine Bowles used to say. Now there are 10 billion in assets for sale and the same group of incompetents is running the show with an approved and improved group of private contractors. After all, using KPMG or any other major financial institution can be a great deodorant. The talent of the private sector will cover up the smell of ignorance and incompetence. To add insult to injury the SBA expected you to work for free, using the "prestige" of working with them as a lure. In fact it was a way to draw blood and accomplish econocide. Always remember, no one is watching them and if there is an investigation there will be indignation and then indifference.

# RECOVERY

I tried to maintain an indifferent attitude towards the loan sale insofar as I was unwilling to participate unless it was as a paid consultant. The weird phenomenon I observed is that anyone will let you work for free. There are many people in the business community that want to pick your brain and promise future rewards and then if you succeed you're not certain to get compensated. Phrases like back end participation or success fees are thrown out there to lure you in, but it's a fool's game. It's better to keep your cash flow in shape because you have to be able to afford the risk that the plans go sour. I learned that the hard way.

Consequently I find the nostalgia approach to give me peace of mind. I have read recently about studies that indicate that victims of diseases are helped psychologically if they write about their experience. I hope the reader will indulge me, I am still suffering from the virus I caught from the shameless personnel at SBA. I don't know what to call the disease but it does exist, perhaps the EPA should do studies to determine the origins of the lagoon disease. I know what to call their strategy: no way out. Washington, D.C. is a town that values indecision and delay and it permeates the private sector that feeds off it, unless you get paid by the hour. The resignation to that way of life is a commentary on the human condition. Lot's of people pulling in thousands of directions. Pressure forces decision otherwise its cover your ass and put the ball in the other guy's court.

Hopefully the loan sale will torment the SBA with demands from reasonable business people who have the leverage to get them out of their torpor. During the first loan sale I contacted a woman owned firm that was hired to make introductory calls. People I had contacted were calling me wondering how they were on the list. My hunch is that the lagoon used my names and then handed them over to the new contractors. I visited the offices of this woman owned firm and it was in an old building in SoHo NY. On one level I was pleased that another small business had a chance to make some money, but I realized the classic reinvent the wheel process was used by the cabal to postpone the inevitable. By the time the new contractor understands the work, they're gone and a new contractor has to start all over again. Remember taxpayers pay for this charade. What was the purpose of this firm calling prospective buyers when they were not brokers? The marketing was like the telemarketers that interrupt everyone's business day. One-sided calls with little follow through, and then they can say they provided notice of the sale. When I was reaching the sophisticated investors on the Bloomberg worldwide, the cabal challenged the wisdom of that but they encourage simple telemarketing? Occasionally I read stories about whistleblowers that reveal fraud in the government and receive part of the monetary recovery. The origins go back to the Civil War but the legislation endured. Unfortunately the whistleblowers can go bankrupt trying to uncover the fraud and are clearly ostracized by their peers. Resignation to the status quo even if it perpetuates a fraud is acceptable because you are a team player.

The advent of e-mail has made marketing cheaper and efficient. It is less intrusive than a fax and it is a way to get into someone's membranes subtly but convincingly. It is a novelty. Unfortunately it wasn't as ubiquitous in the early part of the contracts: 1993 – 1995. I found the worst thing you could do to an SBA employee is throw them a curve. Business as usual was the credo and any disruption was met with wagons circling so fast you thought you were in a Western Movie: Beware Civilians, They Are Doers. You remember that flick?

I even contacted a government accountability project about being a whistleblower as a government contractor, but I think the law requires you to be a government employee to reap the rewards. It is wonderful to believe you can reform the system but all you can achieve is incremental and for the most part you're kept at the edges. I used to enjoy roaming the hallways of the SBA in the early years because I had a sense of purpose, but you were actually alerting them to your presence which gave the advance warning system they needed to create the invisible wall. Smiles and handshakes but nothing moves without their blessing and it's just a matter of time before they torpedo a good idea. I guess some of them spent times on submarines, or sewers.

As of May 1999 the puppets continue to have their strings pulled. The puppets are the private contractors that do the work of the SBA lagoon cabal until they don't like the way things are going.

Then they paralyze the initiative with meetings and indecision and hire someone else to postpone the inevitable: declaring the SBA an anachronism and folding the guarantee program into the Treasury Department. Keeping it alive for under a billion dollars a year is politically safe, but it is spending more money for propaganda than anything else. Prosperity will keep it alive for at least another decade.

The newest puppet KPMG did not seem to know very much about the loans in the sale. Then again, would congress really care about the incompetence of the loan gathering process? The system won't change so perhaps the penetration approach will help to maneuver under the tent. In an effort to bid on the first loan sale it was agreed the best method was to get into the tent and sniff around for information. There wasn't much forthcoming.

Ironically by avoiding SBA s headquarters in DC, I am able to get more reliable information. The level of awareness of developments is low and slow and the quality of the SBA personnel was wanting. There was a general hunker down mentality characterized by fear of new ideas that really paralyzed the staff.

My asset sales project was doomed from the start so why did they bother? Because they had to politically but practically they made sure it would not succeed. Just because they are stupid and they don't like you doesn't make it bad faith. Those were the unforgettable words of Judge Daniels of the General Services Board of Contract Appeals. Essentially I had to show voodoo dolls with pins in them or my burnt effigy or perhaps a tar and feather incident to demonstrate that these lagoon occupants couldn't stand me. The antipathy was coordinated with the program people who oversee the assets and the lawyers.

Gary Fox the litigation specialist was from the shameless school of legal thought. His reaction was always hysteria and overreaction. For example when we discussed document requests he would become flustered and suggest that I was trying to get the entire history of the asset sales by SBA when all I was seeking was the period when I had the contracts. His camel strategy included no break even for water while he took my deposition. The sad part is he viewed his role as a torturer not an interrogator. His suck up associate, David Fishman gave him the necessary strokes to inspire his callousness and feelings of satisfaction at perverting my responses in the depositions.

# REGRETS

It is difficult to look back without feeling sadness and regret. It is years later and I still can't shake the experience. Perhaps I was too single-minded, but as far as I was concerned I had the ability to utilize the Bloomberg, one of the most respected financial information systems, to sell millions of dollars worth of government assets. It was ecommerce before its time. The loss of a 3 percent commission on a 70 million-dollar transaction is not a welcome thought. If the lagoon had negotiated in good faith instead of their head in the sand, stonewall mentality, the sale would have taken place. I can still see the cabal sitting around the table at Washington office of The Carlyle Group. It was a joint effort to destroy a simple idea: sell distressed real estate assets in bulk and lower the costs of carry for the agency.

I receive a pip, property information package from the FDIC with an appraisal attached. So obviously someone selling assets for the government realized the appraisal had the kind of information a buyer needed. But the cabal said no and it was only a matter of time to pass and the initiative would be squelched. It reminds me of the stories of the Soviet Union's decision making process.

The SBA is shameless as to how they are perceived. The lesson from this contract was there was no effort on their side except doing the minimum and whatever they could to slow the momentum.

# OUTSIDERS NEED NOT APPLY

Is there any real oversight by the congress? We don't want no outsiders telling us how to do business is the attitude of the SBA. The goal is to alienate newcomers and the right response is to rebut the Lamar Kelly mindset of we thought you died. I wouldn't want to give them the satisfaction. So I hope the reader is left realizing how sad the state of affairs is at this backwater of a federal agency. Will the lights ever go on at SBA? It's future should be only as a guarantee agency. You can challenge the weakness of their system just by showing up because it is well insulated. Ironically the security system has been beefed up since the early days when I visited. I recall the rapid exit that the head of the FOIA office performed when I asked to see her unannounced. You would have thought I yelled fire. She was the same deft lagoon member who didn't produce my 6-point memo as to why my FOIA request should include a waiver of the processing fee. I remember drafting the memo in a hotel room in Florida and showing to my Dad. He was impressed. I explained that I used the FOIA guideline book to bolster my position. Somehow the memo never became part of the administrative record to be reviewed by the Federal Court even though I faxed it from Florida to the program people, the attorneys, the senior management and the FOIA staff. Convenient amnesia was prevalent.

I am revolted by the gall of the SBA giving out awards for business, they don't understand business, and they understand paralysis. The Four Seasons Hotel was the site of the bid conference for the first asset sale. It was an ironic combination. Most of the SBA staff probably never set foot in the place before. It was at least 85 degrees outside and there was the chief of the cabal, Eric S. Benderson in a 3-piece suit. It would take a lot more to give him dignity. He really looks like Al Capone and would be a facial matchup for one of those separated at birth photos, with Al Capone and his face side by side.

My attitude was to stay in their face at the bidder conference and don't work for free for the potential buyers. At least the incompetents at the SBA paid me but the buyers were only interested in offering equity in the deal or fees at the back end. Unfortunately after surviving the SBA contracts I was not in a financial position to offer my insights for free. Econocide is a devastating event. I didn't have to worry about money until I got the contracts. They use people and then let them bleed to death while they keep the incompetence at full throttle.

The report on the Dept. of Energy after security leaks involving nuclear secrets should be done for the SBA but there isn't a threat to national security, just a perpetuation of national stupidity.

# FREQUENTLY AVOIDED QUESTIONS

By June of 1999 the FAQ's of the SBA's website still left the issue of lender consent unanswered. The lack of definitive positions on this issue illustrates the special patience, even masochism, that is required when you are dealing with the federal agency that flies below the radar screen. Anything less than a billion dollars doesn't matter in Washington. The consent of the lenders should have been resolved and as I have indicated I don't think it was ever an issue. They just use the Fox School of Litigation and raise bogus issues to distract the doers from accomplishing their goals.

For the reader's edification here is the aftermath of my sales efforts in terms of what the SBA is now trying to present: asset sales in the billions. So they committed econocide with me and then proceed to sell loans by giving the buyers the kind of information they refused to give me for my buyers. Doesn't that sound a little arbitrary to you?

# PILOT PROGRAM THWARTED

By the end of the 1994 pilot program it was apparent to me that I really didn't have a product. The database they gave me access to was the same one on their dial up service and ultimately on the Internet. It was pathetic. I believed the expansion of the database information was mandatory and thanks to technology, it could be down painlessly and inexpensively. But if you don't want to launch the rocket all you have to do is hold back the fuel. For me, the fuel was the appraisal information. It was done by independent professionals and it contained the input mandatory for a buyer. The SBA raised the excuse of revealing the dollar value and that it would artificially affect the bid. In truth, it is only an estimate and it is the actual sale that determines value. Robin O. Clay, my contracting officer went "Nelly" on me in his letters that he wrote and Arnold S. Rosenthal signed. Going "Nelly" is what a gay person does when they overreact. I didn't care about Robin's sexual orientation but there was an inordinate amount of spitefulness in his missives. Again the lagoon cheerleaders encouraged econocide; it made their day, even their year. Remember they are lifers, they are not going to make it out of the agency so they might as well destroy you along the way because their outlook is bleak. They hate you for succeeding at doing something they could never do and you don't only need them because they are in the way. When charm fails used the hammer, but the barriers required heavy equipment.

# Ludsin Model Epiphany

---

It wasn't until 1997 that I realized I didn't have a willing seller. In October 1994 I was having a power breakfast with myself at the Sequoia Restaurant in Georgetown. As I sat there trying to enjoy the surroundings I had an epiphany of sorts. Why don't I use appraisals of the properties to describe the portfolio?

I called it the Ludsin Model. We would get appraisals from the deposit paid by the bidders for the COLPUR portfolio. The losing bidders would get the refund of the prorata deposit and the winning bidder would get the deposit applied toward the purchase price. I fashioned it after the concept of ante in a poker game. You had to pay to play. I assumed any purchaser that had the firepower to buy the portfolio they would be willing to put up the funds to get the appraisals and get a refund if they were the losing bidders. It was a no lose situation.

The wisdom of the SBA was readily apparent when E.Granville Craddock asked us at the end of the pilot program whether the SBA could use the appraisals too. Of course he was well aware of the fact that the SBA already had appraisals. The personnel in DC would rather duplicate expenses than reveal information for fear of losing their power. The money they are spending isn't theirs anyhow. Ironically this would not be considered bad faith on the part of government officials. The legal standard is well nigh infraggable proof. Of course no reasonable person would know what well nigh infraggable proof means, but that is the language judges use. They should simply call it the smell test, but that robs them of the mystique surrounding their judgment. One of my favorite responses was from Judge Daniels, the Chief Judge of the General Services Board of Contract Appeals. He said to me during a conference call that just because the SBA staff was stupid and didn't like me, that was not sufficient to establish bad faith. I thought to myself, it was a good start and if I had the opportunity to tell the story he would see it was part of a pattern of obstruction and obfuscation. I used to describe it as a 3-D experience, delay, derail, and defer. The SBA was required to get appraisals annually. So my epiphany wasn't very profound to them.

I also succeeded in getting the databases of the FDIC, RTC, HUD, Defense Department, and the GSA. The concept of brokerage is frustrating because you frequently don't get paid until the transaction is done. So a broker works and if the deal craters, you have nothing to show for it. There are also cases where the broker gets cut back by the parties to the transaction. Consequently, it was better to have the retainer during the pilot program, and even better to have the retainer against commissions for the marketing contract.

# SLEEP BEFORE ACTION

I always entertain myself with new meanings for the acronym SBA. Should Be Abolished, Such Bad Actors, you get the idea. Just for old times sake I called the Boston SBA office to check on a piece of Colpur, no call back. The favorite reply is it's on the Internet, but they overlook the fact that the source of the information is from their office. Thus no accountability when any simpleton can connect the dots and see that garbage in garbage out was the method of information dissemination by the SBA. Thanks to the Internet I can download the basic information that the info retros wanted to hide, but now the train is out of the station.

The story of the Count of Monte Cristo is about the 20 years it takes for revenge. Hopefully the speed of information and the new attitude about reinventing government will bring the changes needed at the lagoon. Otherwise the toxic ooze will permeate the support system that should exist for small business.

I tried to get a form of closure at the prebid conference in Washington DC in June 1999, but it only opened the wounds. The sight of Arnold S. Rosenthal and Eric S. Benderson sitting on the dais was revolting. They would look better in the witness stand at an investigation of their abuse of their positions. Rosenthal was putting the lowest quality loans into the first sale according to Lisa Drazin, another former SBA private contractor.

In the summer of 1999, I dug out the FOIA field list from the end of my appeal file and sent emails about Colpur status to the field. I'm sure I caused a stir because they don't want you to get behind their firewalls. I entertain thoughts about reviving the Colpur project but econocide reminds me how wasteful that is. The SBA still spouts the idiocy of telling me to look on the website for their offerings when it is apparent the info is pathetic. Benderson indicated at the pre bid conference in DC that there was only 50 million of Colpur left. What is left of SBA when the liquidations end? When I started email Colpur contact effort. The local offices refer you to the website and they are the ones that provide the input. The newest position is to pass off inquiries to the private sector.

# INSANITY

Insanity is repeating the same behavior and expecting a different result. It is comforting not being involved with so much negative energy. One benefit of the SBA econocide experience is the loss of illusions on politics. That's like saying a flood helps you avoid swimming. They take the oxygen out of the balloon and we can only be grateful that the SBA keeps most of the lagoon quarantined in that agency.

Here's an example of the communications to the lagoon:
By Fax and Mail March 22, 1997
Eric S. Benderson
OGC Litigation
U.S. Small Business Administration
409 Third Street S.W.
Seventh Floor
Washington, D.C. 20416

Re: Identification of Chase V. Magnuson as Prospect Dear Eric,

I have enclosed a printout from Volume II from my Annual Written Report, page 286 where I had identified Chase Magnuson as a prospect in an entry dated Aug 27 94. I will forward another identification of his name from the 64 page list I had submitted as a supplement to the Annual Written Report. Chase Magnuson was identified as a prospect during the 1994 Pilot Program and then renewed pursuant to the 1995 which provided for inclusion of the 1994 prospects in the 1995 contract.

Thank you for your consideration of this matter.
Cc. Aida Alvarez, Administrator
David A. Fishman, OGC Lit.
Chase V. Magnuson, Beitler Commercial Realty Services
Peter C. Kane, Kane Corporation
Interpretation: I would only be paid in the year after the 1995 marketing contract if I identified the prospect during the contract period or names carried over from the pilot program. One bidder was Chase Magnuson of California. I dubbed him Superman, because he delivered on of the early bulk bids following the first escrow deposit by CS First Boston in December 1995. So the SBA was practicing their usual obfuscation by forcing me to identify the potential buyers. I was able to do that because of the constant record keeping, but they should have been grateful for any bidder, new or old.

Nixon said don't hate those that hate you for you destroy yourself. I came into this process with energy and commitment and left discouraged and depressed. Perhaps it was my form of public service, but it's too high a price. I was naïve about Washington because my experience as a member of the U.S. Holocaust Memorial Council made me believe that things were possible. Instead my experience memorializing genocide gave me confidence to pursue a money making concept that lead to my econocide. They love to put the cheese in the trap and then change their mind. You would think they personally own the assets. After the SBA shatters a life can there be retribution or a balancing of the scales? They say you don't have to murder someone committing suicide. Perhaps the SBA's cavalier behavior will lead to their implosion. After econocide maybe we'll be blessed with bureaurocrocide. A bureaucracy that turns on itself and collapses of its own bloat and decay.

I tried to turn a negative into a positive and became the Hewlett Packard poster child for using their equipment to sell the portfolio. It was a true accomplishment in the art of spin. I am haunted by the calculated plan to delay and scuttle the bulk sale. I can't go quietly into the night. Being deprived of 1.4 million dollars doesn't leave one with a great taste. The possibility of publishing a book rekindled my desire to tell the story of the contract from hell and it is fitting I rededicated myself on the third anniversary of the bids in 1997 and the loss of my father. His loss was devastating for me and I hope the spirit of persistence and optimism will carry me beyond econocide. After all, my mother survived the genocide in Nazi occupied Latvia during World War II and my father got out before the war and started again in America.

Who was Barzini? Barzini was one of the heads of the crime families in the Godfather who undermined the Corleones. I think it was Benderson who is the least principled of the cabal. He would go to any lengths to cover up the incompetence of the agency. That's a lot of work.

Have all SBA contractors been hung out to dry? I called David Fishman to get a list of SBA contractors. His reply: they don't keep a list of contractors. Isn't that a little surprising that they don't have the list of private contractors? Stonewall first and keep the walls up.

# MISSION FROM MARRED

Writing this book is a duty because of the petty disgusting antics of the mission from marred. Since reinventing government is really a power play is it worth exposing venality. I think so.

I reviewed the experience by starting with Volume 1 of the Annual Written Report. I was embarking down a road of no return when I filed the FOIA lawsuit. I was proud of myself for acting and I was more confident about my understanding of the Freedom of Information Act. It is a wonderful law. Unless there are 9 reasons to keep the information from you, the government must give you the requested data, but they can charge you for it, which is exactly what they did to me in order to stop the progress.

I have used the Volumes as a frame of reference and in the words of Guy Gugliotta, the reporter for the Washington Post who wrote about my saga, talking to Ludsin is like walking in to the middle of Gone with the Wind, you don't know what's going on but it is certainly epic. Accordingly, I am reminded of my interactions with the Assistant U.S. Attorney. She was serious and although I tried to use blarney and reason, she was doing her job. Fortunately she was a buffer between Eric Benderson and me.

He is your garden-variety snake. I remember our first appearance before the magistrate when he casually leaned back and asked whether I am incorporated or a sole proprietorship. I responded that I was a sole proprietorship, which meant I could represent myself. The magistrate was sympathetic and he basically said less is more, which was his polite way to tell me to shut up. He ordered the SBA to provide the appraisals by January 1, 1997. Of course that was a 6-month delay for purposes of selling the properties but it was progress. I only had one year after the contract and the SBA took the position the contract was over in June 1996, but that was inaccurate.

In addition, they are so programmed in their response that it is usually the same no matter what the facts are. I recall the tactic of exaggeration was a regular method. Gary Fox was a seasoned practitioner. He tried to raise a kind of domino effect theory to create fear that the SBA would be besieged if the goal I set out for myself was met. For example, when I was trying to explain the marketing approach I took and how I put down names of a wide cross section of people or companies I solicited in my travels he would jump in with the hysterical fear that I could have put down everyone in the phone book and they would not have known the difference. I immediately thought how absurd this reaction was and yet it was their tactic to exaggerate and belittle your legitimate efforts by overstating the worst case scenario and creating fears that were groundless.

# ANNUAL WRITTEN REPORT

My Annual written report was 6 volumes and 1200 pages long. It was my impression that it would be important as a litigation document. It's hard to be chronological particularly when your subjective but I could not make it up. How did the SBA go from 400 properties to 99? Was there perjury by the OPM (Office of Portfolio Management) staff on the issue of their knowledge of the bulk sale and the structural impediments to that transaction?

The intransigence and convenient amnesia are what galls me. The agency is a relic that is window dressing for minorities and disadvantaged and women. It is a cabal with the likes of Benderson in charge, and someone should tell the public what miserable people administer the SBA before others get caught in the web of econocide.

# FIVE YEARS IN LIMBO

In my first appearance before Magistrate Peck in the FOIA fee waiver claim, I sensed the Magistrate was thinking there but for the grace of God go I. His observation from the bench to shut me up was "Less is more". Susan Baird, the Assistant U.S. Attorney was polite but was doing her job to make it difficult for me to enter the court. She challenged my right to proceed pro se, as in fool for a client by being your own lawyer, but subsequently dropped the objection. It was useful to have her as a buffer and ironically my earliest forays into Federal Court were fairly successful considering that I received 75% of the appraisals without paying the $10,250 fee the SBA invoked to break my momentum. The fee was discretionary, they didn't have to charge it, but they were being their petty, spiteful selves.

As I was challenging the SBA to cooperate I discovered they were doing a study to determine the value of their assets. Woodmont Asset Management was a firm organized by Lisa Drazin. She had experience with some federal agencies. She was keeping her study private. Originally the SBA was going to pay her $350,000 but that was reduced to $150,000. I was troubled by the fact that Colpur assets were part of the study. Instead of cooperating with me to actually sell the real estate portfolio, they were spending more time and money to figure out what it would be worth in theory. Why bother? After all as another investment banker friend observed the portfolio I was trying to sell was a pimple on the ass of an elephant, the elephant being the Federal budget.

Everyone asks why did the SBA thwart me. Answer: 1 million dollars. I realized I was finishing this saga during the Los Angeles Democratic Convention in August 2000. It is distressing to think I spent most of the last 8 years pursuing the dream of selling the SBA assets on the Bloomberg and then watching the idea explode in my face. I pray that my experience will be a warning to others, stay away from this federal agency for fear of econocide. The stench of truth should be sufficient warning, but if you missed the point, I repeat, let this lagoon evaporate.

After viewing a report on ABC on April 5, 2000 about red tape I was prompted to write this piece:
ABC Pitch
Freedom from red tape makes countries rich and too much regulation makes them poor.

Although foreign countries have barriers to doing business it should not be a surprise to learn that we have similar problems in Washington.

Steve Ludsin thought he could accomplish a simple goal: sell the real estate of the U.S. Small Business Administration that involved 400 to 500 properties nationwide. The properties were collateral for small business loans. He believed the Clinton Administration's call for reinventing government, helping small business and using the information highway. He thought the idea of placing the photos and appraisals of the real estate on the Bloomberg and attract bulk bids for the whole portfolio was a good one.

What he discovered is the harsh reality that the "lifers" at the federal agency created to assist entrepreneurs was able to stall any new ideas by remaining mired in intransigence and delay. The contract came into being when Erskine B. Bowles was Administrator of the SBA in the beginning of the Clinton Administration. He understood the benefits of the electronic marketing idea and gave the approval in 1993. After the 6 month pilot program, Steve Ludsin succeeded in getting a one year renewal despite institutional resistance. It took 8 months to get the renewal. Steve Ludsin was a delegate to the White House Conference on Small Business from Manhattan, N.Y., sponsored by Congresswoman Carolyn Maloney.

We have inured ourselves to listening to the propaganda of the SBA without seeing the hypocrisy. The main goal of the "lifers" is to perpetuate their power. The sale of this real estate portfolio would be a minor part of the budget and would free up funds and personnel to focus on the guarantee programs of the SBA.

One glaring example was the need for Steve Ludsin to resort to the Freedom of Information Act to get the appraisals of the properties he was hired to sell. SBA invoked a $10,250 fee which they had the discretion to charge, but it wasn't mandatory. The use of the regulation was to slow down the momentum. Steve Ludsin succeeded in getting 3 bulk bidders including the prestigious

Carlyle Group in Washington, D.C., which includes former Secretary of Treasury James Baker and OMB Chief Richard Darman, among others. The SBA waited until 2 years into the second contract to inform the bidders that SBA needed the approval of the lenders before they could sell the properties. Again the regulation they relied on was not clear on this issue, but when they want to stall and pervert the process they can take questionable positions and force the private sector to waste time and money removing obstacles unnecessarily imposed.

The SBA is under a Congressional mandate to sell the loans to the private sector. The first sale involved about $350 million in small business loans. Steve Ludsin tried to form a buyers group to buy the loans but was unable to do so. When he attended the bidders' conference he was sickened by the fact that the SBA willingly supplied the appraisals from the loans in this $350 million loan sale, but refused the same documents for his $60 million real estate sale. The commission for the real estate sale was contractually determined to be 2% to 4 % of the value of the portfolio, which would have been $1.2 to $2.4 million. So red tape destroyed this profit opportunity, because of the arbitrary acts of the "lifers". The mindset of regulators isn't confined to developing nations. Just take the Metroliner to Washington.

Along the way I would try to dramatize my plight the White House as a reminder of how the lifers in the lagoon destroyed my life. After all, I recall Erskine B. Bowles immortal words to me as I walked with him in front of the White House," Steve, I don't like the way they treated you over there." There was the SBA lagoon, home of pond scum and even lower forms of life.

January 16, 1998
President William J. Clinton
The White House
1600 Pennsylvania Avenue N.W.
Washington, D.C. 20500-2000
Re: Catch 23
Dear President Clinton,

It couldn't help but notice that Administrator Aida Alvarez followed you out of Air Force One when you came to New York yesterday for the Wall Street event. I saw the news coverage on television and I think the effort to include minorities on Wall Street is a laudable goal.

Perhaps the next time Administrator Alvarez travels with you I would like to know her response to the inquiry as to what policy is being furthered by the resistance to the initiatives I have navigated through the SBA. The Catch 23 referred to above is the nagging question as to why SBA withheld the knowledge that it was structurally incapable of accepting a bulk sale transaction of the distressed real estate portfolio after I spent almost 5 years of my life accomplishing the goal after I introduced the concept to Erskine B. Bowles in May of 1993.

I have become a born again lawyer, which was the last thing I expected when I embarked on this journey into the abyss. They say that in Hollywood they kill you with enthusiasm and in Washington they kill you with indifference. The arbitrary and capricious acts of the SBA personnel have become the basis of my breach of contract lawsuits and the many FOIA claims I had to file. It is troubling that the individuals that your colleague Senator Dale Bumpers, then Chairman of the Senate Small Business Committee, called to task for their conflict of interest in a Senate Small Business Committee hearing in May of 1991 pursuant to an IG report are the same individuals participating in the negotiations of the sale I have tried to consummate under my contract. Eric S. Benderson, Associate General Counsel for Litigation and Walter C. Intlekofer, Deputy Assistant Administrator for Borrower and Lender Servicing lost $11 to $15 million by trying to liquidate assets for the SBA while they were employed by the agency using an entity called EWE as in their initials.

I am totally mystified by the rejection of the Carlyle Group's bid of 60% of appraised value for the entire Colpur real estate portfolio that was generated through the performance of my contract. I know what the skunk at the picnic feels like. I implore you to ethically ask Administrator Alvarez what is the policy that permits this distortion of the process at SBA? I remember our encounter in Hyde Park, N.Y. in February 1993 and how enthusiastic I was after our exchange about the economy and political history.

I would be remiss if I didn't continue our communication and tell you what happens when reinvention of government meets the senior career officials whose only goal is to stay frozen in place. I wish I could be the bearer of better news, but I pray that your Administration can inquire as to why I had to be the victim of a Catch 23 when what I was doing for the SBA was laudable and consistent with the goals of your policy makers. I remain.

Very truly yours,
Steven A. Ludsin
Cc. Vice President Albert A. Gore Jr.
Erskine B. Bowles, Chief of Staff
Stuart E. Eizenstat, Department of State
In an effort to get something out of the disaster in the lagoon I tried a salvage operation and tried to get subcontracts from the contractors on the award list:
November 29, 1998
Chris Hochreiter
Ernst & Young, LLP
1150 18$^{th}$ Street, NW
Suite 500
Washington, D.C. 20036

Re: GS-23F-H0004 GSA Financial Asset<br>Services Schedule

Dear Chris,

I want to thank you for the opportunity to explain my co brokerage approach to your potential contract utilizing the Bloomberg for marketing. I would be interested in working with you and I am a qualified small business for purposes of Federal procurement. I will forward the form you had emailed to me under separate cover.

I have enclosed brochures for your review and I look forward to our future communications, which will hopefully be mutually beneficial. Happy Holidays. I remain.

Very truly yours,
Steven A. Ludsin

# Appeals and FOIA

When I used the FOIA law to get the information I needed, I received letters saying I had not appealed, even when I clearly labeled the requests as Appeals. It doesn't sound terribly important but it demonstrates the use of delay to avoid progress. Therefore I had exhausted my administrative remedies and properly waited for the 20 business day period to elapse prior to filing my Complaint For Declaratory And Injunctive Relief, 96 CIV 2146 (KMW). The SBA Program Office cannot unilaterally characterize an appeal to be a supplement to an initial FOIA request, particularly when the FOIA Chief of the SBA accepted the appeal as of February 22, 1996. She advised me by telephone on March 21, 1996 that nothing would be coming from the FOIA office regarding my appeal. That does not absolve the SBA from its duty to respond to the appeal. On the contrary, I believe the SBA failed to provide an opportunity to provide their own contractor with the administrative relief required under the FOIA statute. They love to ties you up in knots, it's a prelude to the econocide. It reminds me of the cowboy movies where they lasso the cattle and then bring it into the corral to prepare it for the kill. The labyrinth was more complex but the result was the same.

Why does the SBA put up so much resistance to a productive marketing concept that requires a $50,000 refundable fee? Why did the SBA hire another consultant for $150,000 non-refundable fee to do a study of cost recovery of 30 real estate assets I am actually marketing on the Bloomberg, as well as 400 SBA notes, which I could have placed on the Bloomberg and get an actual recovery as opposed to a theoretical cost recovery? Why is the COTR for the Woodmont Asset Management "Study" John R. Cox, Associate Administrator for Financial Assistance, the same individual who has placed obstacles in the path of this SBA Contractor, S.A. Ludsin & Co.? Why does the SBA purposely delay the production of the appraisals for eight months knowing that S.A. Ludsin & Co.'s contract (SBAHQ-95-C0006) will lapse on June 12, 1996?

I had hoped that the U.S. Office of Special Counsel (OSC File No. MA-96-1134) contact: Tina S. Nelson, or the Headquarters Operations Director of the Office of the Assistant Inspector General Jody Newman (Case No.SHL 1400) would answer these questions and realize that the arbitrary and capricious conduct of the Borrower and Lender Servicing Program Office is tantamount to a breach of contract based on an unmistakable pattern of applying a fraudulent double standard to its contractors. Unfortunately you have to get a declaration from the Federal Court that the denial of the FOIA request or invoking the fee was arbitrary and capricious before the Office of Special Counsel will even begin to consider the offenses committed by the federal employees. The fact that the SBA claimed I hadn't exhausted my administrative remedies made a mockery of the process and its own statutory charter to aid, counsel, assist and protect the interests of small business.

The Lagoon is also cheap. If they can stick you with the bill they will. I managed to get the final $1400 they owed me under the contract, but only as the consolation prize in the first ruling by the Board of Contract Appeals.

It was always a simple idea that they complicated because I would have made money. Wouldn't you be angry?

# Time Line

The delay process was poetically described as the time line. As in we won't think about your request for 2 weeks and the time line for a decision is 1 month. Since this was the primary focus of my energy at the time a month was an eternity, but they don't care. It's business as usual, moving 40 mile an hour in the passing lane but they never get a ticket.

I remember going to Florida to visit my parents and I would try to incorporate a search of the properties with my visit. In November 1995 I visited a Sunrise, Florida property from Office of Liquidation portfolio. It was well located and I thought it was a natural. This put me in the hands of the other cabal in the SBIC area. How to get to no was their specialty also. I tried to fold the marketing of their assets from the SBIC program, but they wanted me to do it for free. That was partially my fault, because I suggested including the assets on the pilot program so when the second contract was being negotiated the SBIC staff thought I should work for free until I earned a commission. Fortunately I passed on that opportunity. Since they were committing econocide with 1000 knife and razor cuts, at least I slowed the bleeding.

By December 1995 I had a meeting with Arnold S. Rosenthal, Walter Intlekofer and Robin O. Clay at the SBA headquarters in DC. I was enthused about using photographs and appraisals scanned into the Bloomberg. Fortunately by December 12, 1995 I got a letter of intent from CS First Boston to buy the Colpur portfolio in bulk. When we set up a meeting in January 1996, Rosenthal asked why we were meeting? I was selling the portfolio and he wanted to know why we were meeting. In a harbinger of the stupidity and recalcitrance to follow, they suggested that CS First Boston go to each office and view the assets. Is that the way to accomplish a bulk sale? It was as if the program didn't exist, and in their eyes it didn't. The attorney representing me on the breach of contract action commented I would have been better off collecting my $50,000 retainer for a year and work on other projects because it wouldn't have mattered to the lagoon. In retrospect he was right.

By December 12 1995 I requested the field offices to provide appraisals to Headquarters. I might as well have asked for their secret dossiers because the wall went up. Robin O. Clay started going Nelly on me and the die was cast. There wasn't going to be any cooperation beyond getting photographs. The appraisal information wasn't in the contract so I was out of luck. Of course I was hired because I was unique, innovative and original, but they were never going to accept a new idea. Too challenging and it might have led to success. The stench of truth is flagrant.

By December 12 1995 the government furlough created by the conservative Congress meant the SBA was closed. So I tried to keep working to keep the momentum, but the time was lost forever. This was a critical phase because we had a buyer, but the furlough and the holidays brought things to a halt, which wasn't much of a change from the lagoon's perspective.

I remember Christmas Eve 1995 and I faxed requests to field offices to get photos and appraisals. Fortunately, some offices responded, but most didn't. The appraisals were terrific documents. Everything you needed to know but were afraid to ask. As soon as the cabal got back, they closed the pipeline, so I invoked the freedom of information act and then they had me where they wanted me. First they X-ray you to death and then they say you're too radioactive to deal with. Econocide at its best.

In spite of all the obstacles I was able to get 2 competitive bids and in an effort to get an asking price I wrote to my first contracting officer on June 11,1997:

Jane P. Butler
Acting Associate Administrator for
Financial Assistance
U.S. Small Business Administration
409 Third Street S.W. Suite 8300 Mail Code 7881
Washington, D.C. 20416

Re: Sale of COLPUR

Dear Mrs. Butler,

I am grateful for your June 5, 1997 response to the current offers from CS First Boston and The Carlyle Group. They have submit-

ted the price of 50.66% of appraised value and since you have deemed that offer unacceptable, it would be extremely helpful for you to propose an asking
price that would be acceptable to the Agency. Please contact me at 516 329 5609 to discuss your response. You can also reach me by fax at 516 329 5696 or 212 319 3264.I remain.
Sincerely,
Steven A. Ludsin

David Arzi, Director, Principal Transactions Group Lacy Rice, The Carlyle Group

# THE FIRE NEVER GOES OUT

To the Editor,

I was impressed with "A Forefather of Venture Capital" in the Callings Column by Laura Pederson-Pieterson, April 16, 2000. Alan K. Ruvelson was a pioneer and deserves credit for capturing the spirit of the newly formed Small Business Administration in 1953. As one of the fathers of venture capitalism I think he would be disturbed by his progeny.

I also had a passion that I believed could be directed through the SBA. Unfortunately I encountered a sinking ship. Mr. Ruvelson was creative to turn small business lending upside down. Investments made in exchange for equity are preferable to loans made in exchange for collateral. Being a pioneer means you have to make mistakes but my mistake was trying to work with the SBA. My money making idea involved the bulk sale of the loan collateral for failed SBA loans using ecommerce concepts on the Bloomberg. In 1993 I approached the SBA when Erskine B. Bowles was the newly appointed Administrator of the SBA when the Clinton Administration took office. I didn't realize that the SBA is a relic.

1953 marked a period of promise in post war America. The Small Business Investment Companies program was a laudable concept. Forty years later I speak from bitter disappointment and tell other small businesses stay away from the SBA. Like the rooster in Seinfeld, the SBA is a lean, mean pecking machine. I believed the Clinton administration's commitment to reinventing government, reducing the deficit and using the information highway to improve the economy. In that spirit I conducted a 6 month pilot program in 1994 to sell real estate loan collateral for failed loans on the Bloomberg. I needed more time to complete the project so after 8 trying months I negotiated a follow on one year contract. In order to conduct this ecommerce project I needed the real estate appraisals and photos of the properties to enhance the marketing. The SBA insisted on charging me a $10,250 fee under the FOIA laws which they had the discretion not to charge. I challenged the fee and had to use the law degree I didn't expect to need after 20 years since graduation. We brought the case to the U.S. Supreme Court. I also became mired in breach of contract lawsuits for the damages caused by the SBA's bad faith.

I have learned that anything below 1 billion dollars in Washington doesn't matter. The SBA budget is just shy of 1 billion dollars. The SBA should be revamped and confined to loan guarantee programs and the SBIC program. Congressional oversight is perfunctory. Ironically when I tried to initiate a similar ecommerce program with SBIC assets, the liquidation office insisted on a $21,000 fee. In their usual Catch 22 fashion if you had a contract to sell loan collateral you were a commercial requester so SBA charged you a fee; if you didn't have a contract to sell SBIC assets you still had to pay a fee. The SBIC program people were willing to have me include my services for free while I was setting up the related loan collateral bulk sale but they never hesitated to charge fees. It's hard to be a dollar a year man in today's economy.

I salute the pioneer spirit of Alan K. Ruvelson but that spirit is dead at the SBA and it should be reincarnated. The examples of Silicon Valley and the venture capital investor community are so vital to the success of the hi-tech industry and they should be emulated. The SBA has lost its rudder and is basically a public relations vehicle. Although I am a Democrat, I now understand the Republican instinct to just close an agency that has perverted its Congressional mandate. They picked the wrong target when they chose the Department of Education, they are off by one block: go past 4th street and D to 3rd street and D. Congress can save almost 1 billion dollars and close the SBA. They can keep a few sensible programs and fold them into the Department of Commerce or Treasury. Hopefully the loan sales conducted by the SBA may be the beginning of the dismantling of the SBA. Don't stop there. Perhaps the Department of Navy should be involved or the National Oceanic Administration because the SBA is like the Titanic, a sinking ship hit by the iceberg of intransigence and incompetence. The fifties was an idyllic time but not unlike us baby boomers, its time to grow up and consider retirement. The SBA should be salvaged for its few valuable programs and the rest should be placed in a museum for outmoded business methods. After all we still marvel at the tall ships even though we have ocean liners. The SBA sank years ago its just that no one noticed except us passengers and what is left of the crew.

The contract for the bulk sale of the real estate would have earned me a respectable commission but the crew at SBA resented that profit motive. There were no lifeboats when I decided to jump ship. I swam back to

shore and amazingly I retained enough strength to write a book about my experience, "Clay Pigeon, Fools for Clients" to warn other hapless small business ventures thinking of dealing with the SBA. I say bon voyage and take a lifeboat because you may not make it back. If you don't believe me look at http:members.aol.com/saludsin

# Happy Trails To You

I could probably write 500 pages of the head bashing one experiences in the miniature golf version of World Wrestling Federation channeled through the lifers at the SBA. Suffice it to say that I hope someone reads this and drops all notions of improving government at an agency like the SBA. They are living in isolation and mediocrity and proud of it. If you sleep with dogs, you get fleas, I'm still using bug remover.

Perhaps this experience was meant to revive my writing skills. It doesn't make sense, but I hope the reader stays far away from the lagoon, you'll never be the same once you enter the House of Horrors, so go to the bumper cars, it's more fun and it won't leave scars. Econocide is deadly.